Dedication

This book is dedicated to the 'Sold frontline; Niggas that spent count that bag. I am also dedicating thi "MH" Hall, Mike Williams, Terol Gedonio Martin.

Also, I gotta dedicate this to all the homies locked up in the 'Belly of the Beast' – Keno "Uptown" Wallace, My Big Homie – Antoine White, A Real DC Veteran – Leslie Morris Bridgeport, CT – DC Fat "Kevin Jackson", True Blue, Lil Rico, and to all the Lifers still in the fight.

Last but not least; I dedicate this to all the people that supports the King & Queen Movement. *"This is for us."*

3

Acknowledgment

This one is for all the real ones, all the Kiko's and the Greats!

For Hartford, Connecticut, Highland Park, Michigan – Detroit, Michigan! For Edgewood Street, Cabot Street, Geneva Street, Albany Avenue.

For all the ghettos and hoods around the world! For all the Thousandair niggas trying to get that bag right.

For God's Todd Artis, Jerkeno Wallace, Tafawa Thomas, Neville Thomas, Matthew Thomas, Aswad Thomas, Von Thomas, Shanell Thomas, Queen G, Jeaneen Wallace, Light skin Daddy, Herline Hill, my daughters (A'shea and Netha) I love you both, and congrats on your high school graduation. Queen Miya my life.

Mike Hall, my big brother, Gedonio Martin, Mike Williams, Terol Sampson – lil bro, R.I.P

For my mentors: Ollie Nuby, Deron, Juan, Big Will and Hackettfield.

Trisha Cruze, love you Queen, it's been nineteen years of me driving you crazy and you're still holding me down.

Best for the last and forever, my great Tyron Cherez George. Forever my homie, I love you "Fly Guy." You're the first child I embraced as my own. I celebrate your life every minute of the day. We are one, my boy. As long as I'm living, they are going to respect and know you in the building.

KING OF KINGS

HOMICIDE HARTFORD

King Thomas

I'm going to glorify you with my pen, mind and actions. These niggas are going to hate us once I drop Book IV "Papered Up Polo" because I'm going to disrespect niggas and let them know they took my heir away from me.

Niggas hitting me and talking about how they don't know you were with me, but I promise you, they are going to wish they knew. Yo! My heart hurt 'Pup, but I have to hold us down. I'm sure your siblings will prosper and benefit from this little thing of ours. Love you God!

For everyone riding with me, many names I didn't mention because they are so many, and also many that are not worthy. I'll never forget how the fake ones turned their backs on me. That's why I always lived my best life, because I know when a nigga is out of your sight, he's out of your mind.

So, if you fit the fake bracket, don't even holla, keep pushing. Riding the wave is over, got mu'fuckas thinking we are good, but they don't know the real story because I didn't put your ass out there. Loving and liking shit for social media.

You asked for it, I hope you all enjoy Book One of this Six Book series. Coming next is "Baller's Ambition."

"King of Kings Series."

"King Thomas."

"King & Queen Publishing."

Prologue

"What kind of fucked life are our kids living these days?"

You might ask yourself this question a time or two while reading this book. Well, it is what it is. This life is real, and from ghetto to ghetto, all over this country, it's the same damn thing. As a black youth, we're so focused on the "Fast Life" that we are almost programmed to adapt to this very way of living just to survive.

We have to fight our way around so many obstacles in an attempt to escape the Belly of the Beast, and it's always easier said than done. Some of us find the ladder of success and climb for all we're worth, while others are killed at the hands of our own people.

The majority of us, at one time or another, end up falling into modern day form of slavery, better known as the "Prison System." The Government, a.k.a "Master" puts us behind bars just for trying to get by.

We get slapped in handcuffs and chains for fighting for our families in these streets, but Massa's got no problem sending us overseas to fight rich folks' wars. It's a crapshoot, and I've been rollin' the dice my whole life.

I'm a product of my environment, and I've been through it all. I was raised by some of the best, and I've seen the worst of the worst. I grew up fighting for what I believe in, and till this day, I stand by the same morals.

I write this for one reason only – so you will know what we were forced to be in this life, not what we wanted to be. It is so easy to say that we should be in school, or working a legit – nine to five – somewhere, but there aren't enough jobs for us all, and no school teaches us how to stay out of the streets. We're left to school ourselves.

You are about to witness, first hand, life, through my eyes. For the past sixteen years, I've been living in the Belly of the Beast, and I do not want my kids to go through the hell that I have.

My name is King Thomas and, mentally, I am stronger than I have ever been. I'm serving a life sentence and it will never change me. I'm taking on the Government with all I have, and God willing, my appeal will bring me closer to the light.

My family and friends keep me focused, and my two daughters, Skyla and Princess, are my heartbeat. Thanks to their mothers, I am blessed to be someone's father.

Well, enough of me runnin' off at the mouth; let me get down to the business and school you on this street shit. If you can hang with me, I'll see you at the finish line.

- - -

From having dreams of being a baller to living the life of a Hustler, it's been a fight. Growing up, I am the oldest of five sons raised by a single mother. I had dreams and ambition of becoming a

7

successful black man in a world that was often unkind to its youths.

My family moved from Hartford, Connecticut to Highland Park, Michigan, in the late 80's. My four younger siblings and I grew up playing sports with our friends. We were up for anything, but Basketball was everything.

Basketball was my life in the early days. I was a young and hungry hoop-superstar in the making. The older crowd watched me progress and just knew they would have problems with me.

I excelled in every area of the game, and had the ambition to become "That Kid," the one that made it out of the ghetto, and into the NBA. It was around this time that I was blessed to have met a good friend of mine named Big-O.

I first met O when he came home from college, and I thought my life had made a turn for the better. Big-O took a liking to me off the rip. Right away, he saw something special in my game. He took me under his wing and became a big brother to me.

"Dawg, you got the potential to make it out of the hood and go to the pros," he once told me. He always pushed me to stay focused in school and prepare myself to get that *"real money."* Real money was great, but it didn't take him long to realize how determined I was to get that fast money!

The early 90's were a crucial time in the crack era and we wasted no time getting in on the action. We built our foundation on Geneva Street, putting in hard work and getting our side of the tracks on the map. I didn't give up on my dreams of becoming a professional basketball player.

By the time I hit my senior year at H.P. High, I was ballin' in the streets and basketball courts. My name was ringin' all throughout the city. I had it all – money, women, cars, you name it. I was living the life!

At the end of the day, everybody knew that basketball was my true love. I had Highland Park's hoop scene in frenzy. I was leading my high school team on the court, and we were having a pretty decent year. I recall telling Big-O that I wanted to make enough money to move my family out of the hood, and one day, go to college to pursue my dream of going pro.

I soon got my wish when I took a vacation to be with my main chick up north in Buffalo, New York. My girl, Tonya had moved there to attend Erie Community College. Tonya was a good girl, and we were in a steady relationship. It was a long distance relationship, but we made it work. She was beautiful, the type of woman any man would want as a wife.

During my vacation, I was approached about playing on a guy's "Hoop It UP" team. "Hoop It UP" is a 3–on–3 basketball tournament that travels State to State, sponsoring games for all ages.

During one of my games, I was playing so well and dominating the opposing team to such a degree that a basketball

9

scout named Calvin Johnson came up to me and offered to help me get into Erie Community College.

I was baffled and thought he was just rambling off at the mouth, because I didn't have a high school diploma, not even so much as a G.E.D. Turns out that Calvin's offer held promise though, and I took him up on it. I ended up staying in Buffalo for the rest of the summer and when school started, Tonya and I were both starting our freshman year at ECC.

In the beginning, everything was good. I was doing okay in the classroom and made all of the basketball cuts. I was almost guaranteed to be the starting point guard when the season starts. Everyone in the city was anticipating what kind of year I would have. All you heard was *"Detroit... this"* and *"Detroit... that."*

Shit! I was chomping at the bit, but also nervous at the same time. Winding down towards the start of the season, my luck changed for the worse, and I was heading in the wrong direction. I was having all sorts of problems. My grades started slipping, I got into a fight with one of my teammates, and that led to me getting suspended from the team.

I got into my feelings and made some poor decisions. I ended up leaving school after my first semester, freshman year. My family moved back to Hartford, CT, and I followed them back to my birthplace.

Chapter One

"Back home, to where it all started" was all I could think of as I got off the flight from Buffalo to Hartford. I had no idea what to expect once I hit the streets. My mind was focused on one thing, *"Get Money."* I had a few dollars in my pocket – just enough to dive head – first into the drug trade, and reopen the first chapter of my life.

- - -

– Years Later –

"Time to get up and get this money!" Those were the first words out of my mouth, as I awoke from a long night out on the grind. *"King! Get up, Boo, breakfast is ready!"* Sky's big mouth was the first thing I heard coming from downstairs.

Breakfast did sound good though, so I hopped out of bed, got myself together, and took a well needed shower. After getting dressed, I headed to the kitchen. Sky had quite a spread on the table and waiting for me – pancakes, scrambled eggs with cheese, tea and buttered toast. I filled my plate with a little of everything and started eating.

I've been with Sky for a minute now; we met about a month after I got home from school. I knew she had to be mine the moment I laid my eyes on her. She was a diamond in the rough, and I knew that I had a winner in her. *"King, you gon' eat, or*

11

what?" asked Sky, snapping me out of my trance. *"Boy, what were you daydreaming about?"*

"You. Me. This life of ours." We talked about some miscellaneous family stuff as we ate. We talked about Skyla, our daughter, and the third party in our family. Skyla's the glue that has always held us together. At the moment, she was over at my mother's for the weekend.

Skyla and her grandma Queen shared a tight bond; they both enjoy each other's presence. My "Little Princess" was eight going on eighteen. After I'd had my fill of Sky's tasty breakfast, I finished getting ready and headed out to start my day, just as I hit the door, my cell-phone started ringing.

"Yo! Who is this?" I said, answering the call.

"This is Meth my G, what's good? Are you stayin' in with wifey all day?" Meth asked with more than a hint of sarcasm.

"Oh yeah? You are funny, Kik. My nigga, I was just walkin' out through the door when my phone started ringin'. Shit, you know your boy got a wifey that cooks and takes care of a nigga."

"Yeah? You are shootin' shots, huh, nigga? Great, ain't no work out here, niggas ridin' around lookin' like fiends."

Meth was out of work and wasn't nobody else on the block pushin' no butter. I let him know that I was on my way out there with a little something to hold us down until I got up with my connect.

12

Meth's my hood-homie for real. I and Kik have been holdin' each other down since I got back on the East Coast. We have been gettin' crazy paper on Edgewood Street, better known throughout the city as "Da Woodz." Along with Meth and me, there was my boy God, and a few others you'll meet along this journey.

- - -

I pulled my blue Detroit Tigers cap down to the left side of my head, as I stepped out into the early morning breeze. It was a nice day and Meth certainly wasn't bullshittin'. The block was off the hook! I almost went into a momentary state of shock, seeing all those fiends trying to cop a hit on one damn block.

I was bum-rushed and started serving the minute my regular sales spotted me. I'm talking no shit, servin' like it was legal out here. I can't say if it was drought season, or what, but it looked like a scene straight outside "New Jack City" and I was Nino Brown, holdin' down The Carter!

I'd made a quick stack by the time I'd made it down the block to see what was good. I saw Meth and God coming out of Carlos's Supermarket and I headed towards them.

"Yo! What's good with you two niggas?"

"Great, you see what it is, shit out here off the hook. Get me right, my boy," said God.

"Word to the Gods, Kik, I told you it was poppin' out here.

Niggas need you bad right now," added Meth.

Meth knew me better than most. He also knew I was holding and would get him and God right. *"You already know I got ya,"* I told my two comrades. *"I got some short shit, but I got a big eight for both of you."*

Within minutes, the block was hit with another wave of customers. I ran through about an ounce just from the time I stepped off the porch. God and Meth ducked off to get right so they could get to the business. My nigga Kat came strolling down the block from Homestead Avenue.

"Kat! What's up with you?"

"You already know," she said, *"I got a buck eighty. I need a quarter."*

"Yeah? I got my nigga. Give me a second to get it." I went to the stash to get my Kiko what she wanted. Kat's one of my loyal friends out here, and it's a fact that, in the hood, you keep the loyal ones close to you.

When I came back up front with Kat's work, she and I found ourselves directing traffic, catching the sales as they pulled up. My name was ringing throughout the city, and I was seeing some good money in these streets.

Everybody, I mean everybody in Hartford either knew me, or had heard of me, or wanted to be me. All the niggas I was fuckin' with heavy were gettin' to that bag, one way or the other.

Twenty minutes later, Meth was back from around the corner and diving, head-first, back into the action. *"Yo! That's me right there, Kik! That's my boy!"* Meth shouted. I couldn't help but laugh at my nigga, and I fell back and let him get that paper.

"Great, this shit rinsing!" I told Meth.

"Nobody can't have no work out here."

"I told you that on the phone, King. You thought I was just rappin?" He replied.

"No Kik, it wasn't that. It's just been a while since shit been this wavy. The last time it was this tough, it was '95, and I was in Highland Park, kickin' their ass."

"I'm hip, Great, but what's up with the connect?"

"Meth, I'm waitin' on that nigga Tiger to hit me as we speak. I already know shit gon' be lovely for your boy."

"But how are you sure that kid Tiger is gon' be good, knowin' niggas screaming it's tight out this bitch?"

"I know my nigga Tiger. Trust me, he is good. The other day when I saw him, he was heavy. If shit was bad on his end, he would have got at me."

There wasn't any doubting my boy Tiger; homie was supplying over half the work that was hittin' the streets in every city in the state of Connecticut!

"King, I'm gonna hold you to that, and I hope you're right, because it's gon' be a lot of money out here. Yo, but anyways, I hope niggas didn't forget about Doe-Boy's comin' home party

tonight at The Pyramid," said Meth. *"Man, that shit almost slipped my mind. Glad you reminded me because I've got to hit the mall and grab some gear for tonight."*

My nigga Doe-Boy was back out here, and tonight was gonna be big for the homie. Everybody in the 'hood was gonna be there. As long as the guns didn't come out, things would run smoothly and everybody would have a good time. Unfortunately, shit stayed poppin' off at The Pyramid. No guns gettin' upped was gonna be a lot to ask.

My phone rang and I checked it, wondering who might be hittin' me from a New York area code. I answered it, with no clue as to who might be on the other end of the line.

"Rude Bwoy, I and I gon' link you back in a lickle while for some things."

"Yeah," I replied, *"that's what's up. Just hit me when you ready."*

Although, the 718 number threw me at first, I was happy as hell to know Tiger was good. Now all I had to do was hold tight and wait for him to hit me back. I was sober and needed some bud, so I jumped in the Trans-Am and headed straight to Kent Street to see Briggs and Nephew.

Turning down Kent, I spotted them niggas. They were sitting in a Benz coupe. I pulled up, hopped out, and approached Cuzzo.

"Briggs! What's good, cousin?"

"Ain't shit, King, you know niggas be out here gettin' this early-bird money. What's up with you?"

"I feel you, Kik. You know what I'm on early in the a.m., the God tryna cop some fruits."

I pulled two-hundred off my knot of money and asked Briggs to let me get ten 30 bags of that fruity shit. Briggs and Nephew were known to stay with that good shit.

- - -

I ended up cruising around the 'hood in my Trans-Am under dirty-dark tints, with the T-tops off, blowing on that Haze. The volume on my system was up to the max, so the homies on East Raymond could hear me when I turned off Vine Street.

As I pulled up, I was saluted by my young boy, L-Boogie, who was with the kid Lil' Mac. They were posted up, leaning on L-Boogie's whip and blowing on something. The kids Block, Kool-Aid, and Pillz were deep in a Cee-Lo dice game with a few more of the Kikos. Too-Smooth was in the circle, waiting on his shot to shoot the 6-6-4 Block had just rolled.

"Block, what's up with you, playboy? Looks like you and Kool-Aid gettin' all the money around here, let me hold something"

"Man, King. This shit ain't nothin' to a gangsta. Niggas out here fuckin' around, Kik. Shit out here's tough right now. What's poppin' with you? I know you on the map."

"My boy," I said, *"I'm waitin' on my phone to chirp as we speak, and when shit good on my end, I'ma get at my niggas."*

My phone started ringing, and it was right on time. It was Tiger, and he was calling from the same number he'd used earlier. *"Hold up, Block. Let me take this call right quick."* I stepped off and answered the call. *"Yeah. This King."*

"Rude Bwoy, meet me at da Girl's Farm. I'll be waiting on you, star. Me have some things for you," Tiger stated. I could hear loud music playing in the background, so I knew he was already at the club. I ended the call and let the homies know that I was on a mission.

I also let Block know that I'd be hitting him up in a few hours with some good news on some work. The Kikos asked me about Doe-Boy's party, so I told them that Da Woodz was gonna be in the building. After all, my boy was fresh out the joint, so tonight was going to be his night.

- - -

Arriving at the Girl's Farm, I was anxious to see what my man Tiger had for me. As soon as I entered the building, I saw Tiger at the bar with two badass Jamaican bitches. He called out to me when he spotted me.

"Rude Bwoy! Come through."

"Tiger, what's good?" I asked, pulling up to a stool at the bar. *"Shit in the 'hood fucked up right now. I'm tryna snatch up something real heavy,"* I added.

"Sit, my youth. Sit. Let I chat with you for a lickle. Brethren, things gettin' tight, yes. But me have something for da King. Dis should hold you 'til I get back from Yard."

"Yard" was Kingston. I don't know why, but Tiger was headed home. He did say something about some business in Jamaica that needed to be attended to. Before I left, he hit me with two whole birds. He said he'd get the money for it from me when he got back to the States.

Seeing how the 'hood was in drought status and there was no telling how long things would be like this, or even who had some work, I decided to make this one count and squeeze the block for all it was worth.

Chapter Two

I took the back-streets on my way back to the block to put the work up. I spent damn near the whole drive lookin' over my shoulder, hoping I didn't run into any of them crooked-ass cops. I was also thinking to myself that I needed to hit the mall and cop something to wear to the club tonight.

I was bumpin' G-Unit's new mix-tape, and 50-Cent, Lloyd Banks, and Tony YaYo was fuckin' the streets up. The industry was trying to blackball "The Power of a Dollar," so Fifty was going extra-hard. He was showing niggas "How To Rob," on some fuck-the-whole-city type of shit.

I was feelin' homie's grind, because he was trying to get on, and doing what he had to do, to get where he wanted to be. I picked my cell up off the passenger seat and dialed Meth's number.

"Kiko, what's good?"

"Ain't shit, King. What's up with you?"

"I'm coming down the deuce; I'll be there in a minute."

"Yeah? Aight. I thought you ducked off with a breezy, you know how you do,' Cop some fruits and head out to the Hilton with something."

"Nah, I just left Tiger. He hit me while I was on East Raymond fuckin' with the Kikos."

"Yo , yo, yo! What you need? I got you, right here!"

Then a dial tone; One minute I'm kickin' it with this nigga, I hear him flag down a customer, then he just hangs up on me? I turned up the block and saw him and a few other homies gettin' it.

My cell-phone started ringing, but I sent the call to voicemail. Arriving in my backyard, I grabbed the work outta the back and made my way into the house.

- - -

– 45 Minutes Later –

I finally made my way to the Blue House. My backpack was slung over my shoulder. In that backpack, was a half a brick I'd just whipped up. My brother Nelly and Meth were on the couch, playing "NBA Inside Drive" on the X-Box.

"Goddamn, Kik! You said you were comin' around the corner an hour ago. The fuck? You smoke all the bud?"

"My nigga, I went straight to the kitchen to put this shit together," I said, and tossed him the work I'd cooked up. *"Bro, where the Haze at?"* asked Nelly, ready to get high. *"Here ya go, you thirsty niggas."*

Them two niggas immediately dropped their controllers and started splitting open Dutches. While they were rolling up, I made some phone calls to the homies and a few other people I fuck with; people I'd told I have some work for.

First person I hit was my nigga, Block. I had to make sure him and the Kikos from East Raymond was good. He and Kool-

Aid was already on the probe and circling when I hit him. They came right to the spot and purchased a couple of ounces.

Block saw how high the fiends in the back room were off the testers I'd given out; them niggas was high as hell, so he knew the product was A1. Niggas was pulling up to the Blue House and beating the damn door down once word got out. My Middletown niggas came through and hit me in the head for 63 grams.

"Yo, King. You still tryna hit the mall, or what?" asked God.

"You already know, God. It's twelve o'clock right now. We can ride out in, like an hour."

I took a few more orders then went up the street to my house so I could put some money up. As soon as I walked in the crib, my Little Princess Skyla came running out of her room.

"Hi, daddy!"

"Hey. What's up, big girl? I thought you were staying over at grandma's house for the weekend."

"I am, daddy, I just came to get some clothes for when we go to the park."

I walked into me and Sky's room, and found her relaxing on the bed and blowing something exotic.

"What's up, Sky? I just got ambushed by Skyla."

"Oh yeah? Well, her ass is getting on my fucking nerves. Yo damn daughter had me drive all the way over to Queen's house to pick her up and, when I get over there, this Daddy Lil' gtheylwas

all 'bout how she needs some more clothes to wear. Now, if her ass woulda told me that on the damn phone, I could've brought her some clothes with me."

"She gets it from her momma. Now you see how I be feeling, when you drivin' me crazy!"

"Boy, please! You can miss me with that bullshit! You be the one tryna drive me crazy with all them bitches you got out there in them streets."

"Come on now, Sky, stop the B.S. I don't know where you be gettin' this stuff from. I don't got no other bitches, and they don't be in my face. They be around my niggas," I said, putting the blame on my boys.

"Well, we gonna see tonight, because me and the girls are going to Doe-Boy's party. So, you better have yo shit together. And don't get nobody fucked up in there," she said, twirling her little ass neck.

"Yeah, okay with yo bad ass. Niggas goin' out to have some fun. You really think I'm trippin' on these hoes out here?"

After going back and forth with her for a few more minutes, I managed to finally put the money up. I went back outside to meet God so we could hit the mall. He was waiting in a snow-white MX. The kid, Solid, was in the back seat rolling up a vanilla Dutch.

"Solid, what it do, homie?"

"Ain't shit, King. Just got out here, and I'm tryna get right, ya feel me?"

Kik wanted to cop an ounce but I told him me and God was on our way out to Buckland Hills Mall, out in Manchester, and that I was gonna have to get his ounce once we got back. He said that was cool, and asked if he could ride out with us.

Kik was one of the "official" niggas from da Woodz, so he knew we'd be with him tagging along. God stopped at the Shell to fill up on gas and pick up some more Dutches. We were blowing up the highway, all the way to the mall, blazing blunts of Purple Haze.

Meth stayed back on the block, hogging up all the sales. He was the type of nigga who'd hog the block when everybody else was out and about, doing other shit. All hustle, all the time. That was Meth. He did give me some cash to pick him up an outfit and a pair of construction Timberlands.

By the time we got to the mall, we were on cloud nine. God was high as a kite, his ass damn near slammed into an all-black Porsche as he was trying to back into a parking space. We got ourselves together enough to make our way into the mall.

The first store we hit up was the Timberland spot where I grabbed yet another pair of black leather Timbos. I couldn't even tell you how many pairs I already owned, but them shits is a must!

God picked out the new Timberlands, the ones with the Shirland inside the boots and also grabbed a pair of the regular constructions for Meth. Solid ended up snatching himself a pair of blue leather Timbs that looked sweet on his feet.

We hit some clothing stores next, found ourselves in the Gucci department store, where God and Solid picked out some exclusive shit and also found something for Meth. Myself? I could not find a single thing that I wanted to rock tonight, so I ended up calling The Wreck Shop to see if my man Mega had any new shit in stock.

Mega let me know about a shipment he'd gotten the night before, said he was sure he had something I'd like. I got off the phone and caught God in one of the aisles with this bad bitch who favored Lisa Raye. Home girl was thick too.

I looked towards the cash register and there was Solid, getting his purchases rung up by yet another sexy-ass sales attendant. Once they finished getting their mack on, we headed out.

On our way out of the mall, we passed by Forever-21 and seeing all them gorgeous snow-bunnies working in there had my homies stuck on stupid. I had to pretty much drag them niggas out to the car. I ain't even gonna lie, I was tempted too. My willpower's just stronger than theirs.

I had God take us straight to The Wreck Shop. Mega must have had some kind of ESP-type shit goin' on, because he had some outfits laid out for me before I even entered the store.

Specifically, he had this black Pelle Pelle jacket that was killin' em.

No doubt I'd be the flyest nigga in The Pyramid tonight. We left the Wreck Shop and were driving down Albany Avenue, when God spotted one of his old bitches who'd moved out of town somewhere.

"Damn, Evette! What's good? Long time, no see."

"Hey God. I been alright. I just moved back to CT from down south."

"I'm still out here doin' me, that's it. You still lookin' good. I'm tryna see what you workin' with," God was goin' in! *"The Great's having a welcome home party tonight at The Pyramid. You should come out and celebrate with us; maybe we can get up afterwards, and get reacquainted."*

"That sounds like a plan. Take down my number, and don't act like you too good to use it, neither!"

"Aight, I'ma get at you later."

The two long-lost lovebirds said their goodbyes, and all three of us watched as Evette walked off, sashaying her plump ass from side to side. *"Damn, God. Shorty holdin' back there!"* praised Solid. *"Yeah, Solid, I'm hip. You know I'ma be all up in that after the club."*

Back on the block, Meth, Prince, and Shiest were rippin' and runnin' up and down the block gettin' that money. Shit was full blast. A couple of my customers were waiting to get served, but when they saw me, they made their way over to God's car.

Meth called me up to the front porch of the Blue House and handed me the $2800 for the work I'd given him earlier. He had a few grams left, but needed to buy some more. I told him to gimme a minute to go and get him right and I also had Solid to take care of.

- - -

Cruising up Mather Street, Forty's cell-phone rang. "*Yo, who dis?*" He answered.

"*Kik, this Cutty.*"

"*Yo, what's good Cutty? What you got going on, my boy?*"

"*Me and Crazy homies just hit the block, where you at?*"

"*I just pulled off, a minute ago. Yo boy headed over to one of my breezy's. You know what it is.*"

"*Oh, yeah! That's what's up. Yo, niggas hitting The Pyramid tonight, you feel like partying?*" asked Cutty.

"*What time?*"

"*About eleven o'clock.*"

"*Yeah, I'm with that.*"

"*A'ight, just meet up with us on the Duece when you finish fucking with yo breezy.*"

"*I'll be back around the way around nine or ten.*"

"*Okay, Forty. I'll see you later kik.*"

27

"One, Cutty," Forty said, closing his cell-phone just as he parked in front of Tatiana's crib on Green Street.

Chapter Three

Later that night, we pulled up to Club Pyramid three vehicles deep and planning on having a good time. I pulled my Cadillac STS into a parking spot close to the front door. God parked his whip alongside of mine, and our whole crew piled out of the cars and made a bee-line towards the entrance.

I spotted a few familiar faces as we approached. There was a long line waiting to get into the club, and we weren't trying to be stuck out here in the open, like ducks. The kid, Gates, was at the front table with his promoting team collecting cash and tickets. He spotted our squad and sent one of his guys to escort us inside.

The Pyramid was packed for Doe-boy's coming home party. The ladies were looking good, dressed in their best attires. I even spotted a few broads I'd busted down in the past, but I wasn't payin' them no mind. Niggas was mean-muggin' all around; not knowing that tonight was not a night to be bluffing.

Doe-Boy spotted us through the mass of partygoers, got up from his table in the V.I.P. section and waved us over. We had the V.I.P. section on lockdown. Homies from around the way united to welcome Doe back home. Every table had Hayes and bottles of liquor on top of them.

Doe greeted us with open arms, telling us how grateful he was. Shit was set up lovely, the dance floor was jumpin', and homies were gettin' their groove on and two-stepping. *"Welcome home, my boy!"* I said.

"Yeah, that's what's up, King. I see you back home doin' yo thing."

"That's what I do, yo, but today is all about you, Great."

"My nigga, it feels so good to see all my niggas here, showin' all of this love."

They'd obviously done some major promotion for this one. There were exotic bitches from everywhere in the spot. You also had homies from damn near everywhere – The Ave, Mansfield, Enfield, East Raymond, the Yard, and Burton Street; and they pooled together almost ten racks for homie.

Doe-Boy let me know that Sky was in the building, and that he'd put her and her girls at a table with a couple of bottles. Even though the club was crowded, I know Sky peeped me and my people coming. She was gonna be watching the kid, thinkin' a nigga was gon' have mad broad in my face.

Havin' bitches around this type of scenery wasn't even my style though, so if Sky wanted to catch me at something, she was gonna have to try something else. She wasn't about to catch me slippin'. I wasn't gonna sweat her ass, though. Tonight wasn't the night for that.

"God! What's the deal, Kik?" I asked. I could see the tension in his eyes. *"Them bitch-ass project niggas in the*

building," he said. *"Kik, them niggas don't want no work. They know what it is."*

God didn't sit well with the enemy close by. This was one of the rare times we all partied together like this. God didn't really even play the club scene, but being as Doe had just touched the streets, he came out.

The infamous Mobb Deep came out spittin' that venom shit from their new album, "The Infamy", and a few other hits like "Murda Muzik" and "The Quiet Storm." The V.I.P. section smelled like a Purple Haze factory.

Niggas on the block relate to *"Murda Muzik, niggas on the cell block,"* I recited, as Prodigy rapped. While everyone was locked into Mobb Deep's performance, I took a minute to holler at God about some plans I had for me, him, and Meth.

It was time for our minds to come together so we could get some real bread. We were talking, and just as I was getting to the specifics, there was a bunch of commotion that erupted on the other side of the club. *"Check that shit out, King. Looks like the Kikos over there gettin' it on,"* God pointed out.

I looked up to see what was going on and spotted Meth, Solid, Cutty, Milly, and Sholta scrapin' some other crew. By the time me, God, and the rest of the Kikos got into the action, bottles were flying, chairs were being swung and, out of nowhere, gunshots popped off.

I pulled out my 40 Cal as I found cover. The club was in chaos, people were trying to get out of the line of gun fire and this caused some people to get trampled over. Nothing like a little gunplay to get a stampede started. I looked around, trying to find Sky, but shit was ugly, and I couldn't spot her. We all fell back and made it outside to the cars, where Meth and Solid were already waiting on us.

"What the hell happened in there?" I asked them niggas. *"King, this lil bad 'PYT' was tryna holla at the kid, when one of those suckas walked up talkin bout why I'm talkin' to his bitch. Kik, you already know I wasn't tryna hear that bitch-ass shit. His peoples ran up, Cutty and them walked up, and shit just popped off."* stated Meth.

I turned to Solid, *"So, who was shooting?"* He said one of the project niggas pulled out a knife, so he upped his piece and shot two of them, hitting one in the shoulder, and the other in the back as he tried to run.

My cell started vibrating in my pocket. It was Sky. *"King, it's me, You alright? What happened in there?"* I could hear the concern in her voice as she started in with twenty-one questions. *"I'm good, Ma. Go ahead home. Once we get shit sorted here, I'll be there,"* I told her. *"Bae, be careful,"* she said, *"I'll be up waiting for you,"* she finished before I ended the call.

I sat behind the wheel of my STS and all I could think about is how crazy shit was in the hood. Niggas couldn't even celebrate Doe-Boy's party without something poppin' off. Shit was bound to start stinking, it was just too many sets in one spot. God called that shit from the moment we first stepped in the club.

When I finally made it home, Sky was sitting on the couch and watching some movie on TNT. I could tell she was still tipsy by the way she was looking at me and when she leaned in to kiss me, I could smell liquor.

"Bae, I seen Meth and Solid talkin' to those girls before them other boys walked up."

"Man, that shit ain't nothin'. Them niggas called themselves tryin' Kik over some bitch. Them cats was feelin' theyselves they were deep. Shit popped off, niggas handled business."

"I was worried sick about you, boy. I'm glad you home now, because I would have been up all night worrying about you."

I took a quick shower. It had been a long day, and the only thing on my mind was sleep; I just wanted to lay up with Wifey and forget everything. I got out the shower, wrapped a towel around my waist and walked into the bedroom to find Sky on the bed wearing nothing but a see-through lingerie set.

I eased up on the bed, removed the towel and showed Sky that I was naked from head to toe. Her eyes lit up like strobes when she laid eyes on my manhood. She jumped on me with an uncontrolled viciousness, thrusting her tongue down my throat.

I wasted no time sliding her panties to the side and letting my fingers play with her pulsing clit. She laid down on her back and readied herself as I positioned my manhood to enter deep into her bliss. *"Ohhh, yesss ...Yes King ...Right there ...That's my spot, baby."* she sighed.

I gave her long, deep strokes. Sky's pussy was the wettest, and she fit me like a glove. *"Sky, this pussy is so good,"* I moaned. After making her pussy cum twice, Sky wanted to ride the dick. Dropping her pussy down on my manhood, she started bucking like a real-live, first-class thoroughbred.

I felt myself swell from balls deep and I knew I was ready to release my load. I started thrusting rapidly upward as she pussy-popped downward and, minutes later, finding our rhythm, we ended up cumming in unison.

Chapter Four

-Sky-

I was stretched out on the bed in the comfort of my hubby's arms. All I could think about was how happy and blessed I am to be with this man who is so good to me and Skyla, our daughter. He's given me everything – a beautiful little girl, a roof over my head, and security. These last ten years have been the best of my life. The phone rang and broke me out of my thoughts.

"Hello. This is Sky."

"What's up, girl? This me, Tela. I know yo ass ain't still in bed asleep."

"Nah girl! I'm up. Just layin' in bed next to King. Why? What's up with you?"

"Girl I was tryna see if you wanted to go get some breakfast and do some shopping."

*"Tela, that sounds good. I need to get out the house for a change. "*Me and Tela ain't been out in a minute.

"You want me to come and pick you up?"

"Yeah, but don't be takin' all day. You know how slow yo ass can be."

Before getting out of bed, I gazed into King's face, watching him as he slept peacefully, looking like Skyla in every way. I laid out a red prada mini-dress and a pair of red bottom

35

heel; then I went into the bathroom and ran me a hot bath. Once I was done with my bath, I gave King a kiss on the cheek without waking him up. I grabbed my car key and headed over to Tela's. When I arrived at her crib, this bitch wasn't even ready and she had the nerve to try and play me like I'm the one that's always taking forever. *"Sky, lemme just grab my phone and my purse and I'ma be ready,"* she said.

We settled on IHOP for breakfast mostly because Tela couldn't stop talking about pancakes and her craving for this or that. Tela was just hungry like that; she wanted to eat all the damn time.

During the drive, Tela wanted to know all of the details of last night's drama, thinking that King must've told me everything. *"Girl, he said some niggas tried to get at his boys and that they handled they business. He wouldn't tell me shit else. You know how he gets about shit that goes down in them street."* I explained to her.

I ordered waffles with strawberries and ice cream on top, breakfast sausages, scrambled eggs, and cheese. Tela's greedy-hungry ass wasn't playin', not one bit! That bitch had a little of everything on the menu to chow down on.

"Girl, yo ass eatin' for two, or what?" I asked sarcastically. I knew she wasn't pregnant, but damn, she wasn't holding back, neither. *"Hell nah Sky, I told you I was starving.*

Plus, I was cravin' this shit. What?" she looked at me crazy, *"A bitch can't be hungry?"*

"I'm just sayin' Tela. You ain't miss a crumb." I laughed. We went to the mall after breakfast. Two shopping freaks, that's what you'd call us. We hit all the hot spots for the most up-to-date shit. Tela was addicted for real; I didn't know anyone who shopped more than her.

She shopped for herself, her daughters, and her babies' father. I ended up grabbing a few things for the house and then I hit the Baby Phat store and bought Skyla some outfits. Time flew, and we were starting to get tired from all the walking.

"Tela girl, my legs are killin' me, and I'm ready to go." I said. *"Yeah girl. I'm done spendin' all my money anyways. I'm glad we hung out, though, since you act like you can't come out and play anymore."*

I had to admit, it was cool to get out and chill with my girl. Since Skyla was born, I'd come to find out that there was more to life than running the streets. Besides, King wasn't having it. I dropped Tela's ass off at her house and then I headed home.

I entered the house and followed the sound of the shower to the bathroom. I entered and started removing my clothes. *"Baby, you want some company?"* I asked King. *"Yeah. get in. You were already goin' to, from the looks of it."*

As soon as I set foot in the shower, my neck and tities were getting sucked on. The more he licked, the harder my nipples got, the wetter my pussy got! King bent me over so he could have easy access to my throbbing kitty cat. He penetrated me with shots to die for and I felt his manhood hitting my spot with every single thrust.

After 20 minutes of hot and steamy sex and me cumming three times, we finally got a chance to actually shower and wash each other's juices off. I slipped into some booty shorts and one of King's basketball jerseys and laid down for some much needed rest.

Chapter Five

Sky done got me started early. She really drained me last night. I finally got myself together to start my day. My mom, Queen was cooking her Sunday meal today. So my plan was to handle a few things on the block; holla at a couple of my niggas and head over to Queen's crib with the family. It was a hot, beautiful afternoon and the sun hit my eyes the minute I stepped out of the front door.

It was only 12:30, but already the streets were packed. Neighbors were out relaxing on the front porch, mowing lawns, kids were playing up and down the block and, as usual, the hustlers were out, full-scale, getting money. And the fiends? They were givin' that paper away!

Walking towards Carlos', I spotted God kickin' it with a few chicken-heads from around the way. *"King, what's the deal with you?"* he asked. *"Ain't shit,"* I replied, *"Just gettin' up from that long night yesterday."*

I'd been out there with God for a few minutes, makin' a few dollars when suddenly, out of nowhere, shit got ugly. The Jump Out Boys hit the block. Luckily for us, they came down the one-way street, which let us peep the move before they could get the drop on us. I slid off into the Blue House until shit died down. God hit the yards to get to the deuce where his whip was parked.

– 4.00 p.m. –

Shit finally died down. I made my way over to my mom's crib and arrived just as her and Skyla were finishing their meals. *"Hey, ma. What you got going on up in here?"* I asked, giving her a hug and a kiss.

"King you know we cookin' the Sunday dinner. We gon' have everything. Skyla made today's menu."

"Skyla, what's up? I see you got it smellin' real good up in here." I said to my little princess.

"Daddy, I had Granma make everyone's favorite food." Skyla stated.

Queen said all my brothers were downstairs along with Shelly, so I headed that way. When I got down there, I saw that everyone was in their own world – Shelly was on the computer, Vince, Lil-D and Max were playing PlayStation, and Prince and Nelly were in the back of the basement blazing away on some Purple Haze.

"Damn, Prince. That shit smells fire! Where'd you cop that from?" I asked. *"I went and saw Bizzy before I got over here,"* Prince replied between pulls. We got high and played video games until it was time to eat, and Skyla, Amy, and Lil Nelly brought their nosy butts downstairs.

"Everybody! Food's ready!" yelled Skyla, acting the part of H.C.I.C (Head Child In Charge). We all rushed upstairs, ready to eat and get full. When I got upstairs, I noticed that Sky was

already seated at the table; I planted a kiss on her sweet lips as I pulled up a chair.

The food hit the table, Queen said grace, and everyone dug in. Things went smooth, the kids had a blast; it was a perfect Sunday meal with loved ones. After dinner, everybody hit Keney Park for a day out.

I wanted to hit the block and chill with my boys, but Sky objected to that and convinced me that we didn't spend enough time together anymore. Me being sensitive to her feelings, I caved and decided we'd spend the rest of the day together, just the two of us.

We left the house with plans of hitting the theater in East Hartford to catch a new release. Sky popped in Avant's newest CD and we drove down Tower Avenue listening to it. I heard a loud poppin' noise over the music but didn't think much of it. Not until something hit my driver's side mirror.

Seconds later, the rear window shattered and the whip took several more bullets to the trunk and back windows. *"Sky! Get Down!"* I yelled as I floored the gas and tried to maneuver us out of harm's way. I made a sharp right turn onto Main Street, keeping an eye to the rearview to make sure that there weren't any cars behind us trying to finish the job.

It looked like we were in the clear, and luckily, we were unharmed and had made it through the ordeal without as much as a scratch. I couldn't say the same about my mental, though. I could barely contain my rage. I could not believe that someone tried to get at me while I was out with my wife.

I pulled up on Da Woodz, and as soon as Shiest, Milly and Cutty set eyes on the ride, they could see that something bad had gone down. They rushed over and asked about what happened, asked if we were okay.

Physically, we were fine. My homies could see that. They could also see that Sky was hurting emotionally, and that I was hurting for her. I was from the streets; I was in the streets, so I knew the risks and the danger that came with this shit.

Sky, though? She never asked for this. She was innocent, she shouldn't have been anywhere near the gun play. Her only crime was being associated with me. The next few hours saw us posted up in the back of Moosey's crib, politicking and trying to figure out just who it was behind the botched hit.

I was making calls, Milly was making calls, and we were all just trying to find out something; anything! *"Kik, I bet it was those project niggas from around the way. King, I swear it had to be those ma'fuckas. Shit! Ain't no secret we beefin' with them faggots,"* Cutty said, stating what were starting to seem like facts.

Shiest's NexTel started chirping and it was one of his peoples from the projects, with some info for him. Told him the young niggas from the projects was runnin' around screamin' that they just hit up some kid named King. Also said he heard the shots and saw the boys runnin' back into the projects from Tower

Avenue. Shiest thanked his source and promised that niggas owed him one.

Me and the Kikos agreed that tonight, we were gonna blow through the projects and lay everything down. Before all that though, I wanted to go by the crib and check on Sky to make sure that she was okay.

When I got home, I found Sky on the phone with her girl, Melody. *"Girl, let me call you back. I think I hear King coming."* She hung up when she saw me come through the bedroom door. She was still a little shaken up and it was finally starting to dawn on us just how lucky we were.

That shit could've easily gotten a lot uglier than it did. What if Skyla would have been in car with us? The thought of losing either of them sent my mind into overdrive and had me wanting to kill anybody and everybody involved with this shit.

I spent a few hours comforting Wifey, all the while, my mind working overtime and my heart and my soul wanting payback. *"Sky, I gotta go handle some things. I'll be back later tonight."*

"King, be careful please," Sky pleaded. *"I will. You ain't gotta worry about me,"* I said, *"Things gonna be alright."* I hit up Meth and God and let them know what was going down, and they were ready for war. I got off the phone and went down-stairs, where Shiest, Cutty, and Milly were already strapped and in "Go-Mode."

43

We were two cars deep, heading up Barbour Street when we spotted a group of niggas hustling out in front of the corner store outside of the project. We got up on them niggas and judging by their slow reaction to what was going down, we knew they didn't know that we'd gotten the drop on them until we jumped out in front of the store, guns blazing, trying to kill everybody who looked suspicious.

Despite the slow reaction on their part, they regrouped quickly, and we had a good, old-fashioned, gunfight right there on the street. From every direction, it was heavy gunfire and the muzzle flashes had the streets looking like the Fourth of July.

We heard the police sirens getting louder, and that was our cue to get the fuck up out of there! As we hopped back into our vehicles, I could see a few individuals laid out on the pavement. I wasn't sure if there were any casualties, but I was positive them niggas felt the aftermath of what they started when they tried to take me out of the game.

Chapter Six

-Prince-

Prince makes his way out the bathroom and walks over to Jada, who is laid out sexily on the bed. He doesn't say a word to her, just gets between her legs, kissing the core of her pearl. He then splits her lips apart, tentatively licking her pussy. He sticks his tongue up under her clit, flicking it furiously. She moans and rests her thick legs up over his shoulders.

Prince pushes her legs back even further with his hands and buries his face between her thighs again and continues to give her what she's been craving. Coming up for air, he slips two fingers deep into her pussy and dives, tongue first, into her cunt again.

She gasps and he raises his head, looking into her dreamy eyes. *"You love this shit, huh?"* She bucks her hips into his fingers. *"Yeah, that's it beautiful. Let daddy see how wet this pussy get ...Cum for me."* He wraps his mouth back around her pussy and sucks the juice out of her. He couldn't lie; her petite ass got some sweet, creamy pussy.

"Boo, slow down. Please. Let me satisfy you. Lay back and let a bitch give you some of this slow neck." She raises up and straddles his manhood a few times, trying to bring it to a full erection. She smiles at his size, positioning her face at dick level.

45

She presses her lips to the head and starts planting soft, wet kisses all over it. *"Yeah, that's it baby, suck it just like that."* She swirls her tongue around the head then swallows it whole. He takes a deep breath and licks his lips. *"Damn, ma! Suck that shit,"* he says, guiding his hand to the back of her head, *"Massage my balls, ma."*

She cups his balls and twirls him. The sensation of her sucking and fondling was taking him to the peak of pleasure. She was trying to suck and squeeze the nut right out of him. And she did. His nut shot out like water from a fire hydrant, roaring at the ecstasy she was giving him.

She slurped until he was drained dry, then like a pro, she began to lick and nibble him until he was hard again. Jada got on all fours and Prince leapt on to her back and pinned her hands to her waist. He used his right knee to part her legs and held her in place with his hips.

His manhood slipped down and rubbed against her hairy entrance, making her back arch. She turned around at that moment so she could look into his eyes. He kissed her deep and long. Without warning, he thrust his rock hard pole into her pussy.

Jada moaned as he penetrated her roughly but sensually. His sex felt so good, so right. Every time they made love, it was the best she'd ever had. No man ever made her pussy feel as good as Prince did. As his strokes picked up, she moved her legs even farther apart and moved her pussy to the same rhythm he was moving to.

They both felt their release coming from deep within as they seized up at the same time, and in the midst of her climax, she locked her pussy-muscles around his cock and greedily pulled the nut out of him.

Just like that, it was over. Prince leaned in and planted a wet and sloppy kiss on her lips. *"Just lay back and rest, my love. The night's far from over."* He gets up and walks away from the bed. *"I'll be right back,"* he says over his shoulder, *"I gotta drain this hose."*

- - -

Early Monday morning, I was out on the block getting some more of that early-bird money. I'd been out since 3 a.m., going back and forth from Sigourney and Da Woodz, catching every customer that came through.

I had a few runners, Cliff, Chunky and Cheddar, who were helping me with all of the orders. Where all of these fiends were coming from, I had no idea. I wasn't gonna complain though, they were spending hundreds at a time. The money was coming in so fast that I couldn't even count it!

Meth pulled up in his Mazda around 8 a.m. As soon as he pulled in and parked, he got bombarded by a crowd of customers that all seemed to hit the block simultaneously. From across the street, I screamed out to let him know it was like that out here this morning. Slowly but surely, homie after homie started pulling up on the block until everyone was out and about and gettin' that paper.

I looked into the back yard to check on Bruno and Lady, my two Pitbulls. They spotted me and started barking like crazy. When I got back there, I went into the garage, grabbed the bag of Purina and the water hose and went to get them fed and hydrated. Bruno kept jumping up on me and dirtying my clothes.

"Bruno! Get yo' big ass off me, you be playin' too much!" Bruno gave me a mean look and a defiant bark to let me know that he wasn't tryna hear my shit either. After the pups had gotten their food and drink on, I put them on their leashes and took them around the block a few times for some exercise.

When they'd had enough and we made it back to the house, Sky was posted up in the front window waving at us. Lady went crazy when she saw Sky. Many an all-nighter on the block, Sky would be at that window keeping tabs on me, so I knew just how Lady felt.

I got an unexpected call from Tiger while he was in Jamaica. He wanted me to fly down there and fuck with him for a few days. I was kind of surprised and a little amped. I'd never been to Jamaica before, and now would be as good a time as any for me to visit where my roots were!

There were a few things I would have to take care of before I left, but nothing that would hinder or keep me from going to see what the Don wanted with me. Around quarter after twelve, I received a call from Doe-Boy.

"Yo, what's up?"

"Kik, this Doe. What's the word, my nigga?"

"Ain't shit, you know me. Out and about this money, why? What's poppin' with you?"

"King, yo boy tryna see you for some work."

"Big homie, you know where I'm at. Fall through."

"Be lookin' out for me, King, I'm on my way right now."

Fifteen minutes later, Doe-Boy and this kid, Cuff, from Mansfield Street were up in the Blue House. Doe put in an order for a big eight and Cuff wanted a zip. We got down to business and, just as fast as they'd come, they were out.

I called Meth into the Blue House, and let him know my plans about going to Jamaica to get up with Tiger. I couldn't give him an exact motive for my trip, hell, I still had no clue my damn self as to what Tiger had planned, but Meth relaxed a little when I assured him my little journey was gonna be all about that paper.

Meth still seemed a little skeptical, though, so I told him that I trusted Tiger with my life. And I did, he's been on the up and up with me since day one.

"Don't worry, Kik," I said, *"I'ma let my pops know I'm going down that way too so he'll at least know what's up if shit*

gets ugly. Also, I'ma leave you with all the work I got left. Just make sure my brothers Nelly and Prince are good. I know you'll get God, but besides that, it is what it is. My connect's sending for me and I gotta go see what's good. This is how a nigga jump to the big leagues and it's my time to shine Great." I concluded.

Now it was time to drop this bomb on Sky. I already knew she was gonna flip out, because she doesn't like surprises. I finished giving her the spiel and she went right out on some *"take-her-and-Skyla-with me"* type-shit.

I told her that it wasn't that kind of trip and that I couldn't mix family with this kind of business. She gave me a look of disgust, a look that she saved for whenever things didn't go her way. Sky knew damn well how I felt about my family getting involved in my street life and after going back and forth on the subject for what seemed like forever, she caved.

We agreed to go get Skyla from Queen's crib and take her to Chuck E. Cheese since it was one of her favorite places. Skyla wore us the hell out after we finished our pizza. She had us playing every game in the place, and ended up winning so many prizes we could barely fit them all in the car.

"Boy, why you on some last minute shit?" Sky asked for the thousandth time. *"This shit just came up earlier today, Sky. It's just one of those spur of the moment things. Ya'll gonna be good, I promise. Meth gonna be around to help you out, and Queen's only a phone call away,"* I said.

It had been a long day of running around and I was spent. I wanted nothing more than to get us all home and put Skyla to bed so I and Wifey could take a shower and maybe have an all-night lovemaking session.

Chapter Seven

It was Tuesday morning, and Sky and I had just dropped Skyla at school. After that, we stopped at Silvios and had breakfast. Just this one time, I decided to go over some specifics about my street hustle and the details about my leaving.

Once I'd gotten Sky up to speed, I had her drop me off at the Blue House, where Meth and God were waiting for me. I left Meth with my business phone and hit him and God off with some work.

I also set aside some work for Prince, Kat, and Nelly, with orders to keep them supplied and working. With everything now in motion, my departure time from Bradley International Airport was looming large.

- - -

When I arrived at Norman Manley International Airport, I spotted a close associate of Tiger's. I'd known him for some time, his name was Poochie. *"King? Whomp, star?"*

"What's good with you, Poochie? Long time, no see," I replied, shaking his hand. *"Respects, Rude Bwoy. The I awaits you, brethren. Him have some good things to chat about. Come, make mi show you Kingston."*

We walked out of the terminal to a caravan of Benzs. I was directed into the back of one and found Tiger waiting for me.

52

"Whomp, me Don," Tiger greeted, *"How was your flight?"*

"Ah man, Tiger. The flight, it was lovely, and you know me, I'm coolin'," I said.

"'Nuff said. Let mi show you what Yard like."

"Sounds good. Oh, yo. Tiger. I wanna check my boy Dilly Dread out Denham Town."

"Who dat? Dilly Twos? Two Time? Yeah, man! Dilly my bredren from long time," Tiger stated.

We rode out and kicked it all the way to Tivoli Gardens. I was looking around the whole time, tryna see what I could see. This was the ghetto for real. Everyone on the streets just looked on as the real shottas rolled through, under the cover of dark tints.

It was at this point that I knew my boy Tiger was really on Don status. He took me to a dancehall party at Rick's Cafe. He also let me know that Dilly was to meet us at the function. He'd had one of his people link up with Dilly Twos and let him know that I was on the Island.

Rick's Cafe was jumping and loaded with artists like Beanie Man, Yellow Man, and Super Cat. Even Bob Marley's two sons Damien and Stephen came through. It was a special night, and me, Tiger, and Dilly hung out the whole night, smoking and drinking Heineken.

When the party died down, I went to Denham Town with Dilly Twos. I got to learn a lot about Dilly's life in Jamaica. I met his wife and children and also came to find out that Dilly was real heavy in this section of Jamaica as well.

In the morning, Dilly took me to downtown Kingston, to Randy's Records, to pick up some of the latest dancehall tracks. I called Tiger around 9 a.m. and told him to have someone pick me up so we could get down to the business.

When the caravan of Benzs came by this time, I could see that Tiger was along for the ride. He took me on a tour and showed me different sections of the Island – Trench Town, and a few others on the west end of Kingston. I imagined living down here when I got older and my paper was right.

I got to find out Tiger had a serious problem here in Kingston and that was why I was here. There'd been a shootout at a kids' party and Tiger's seven years old daughter was shot and severely injured. Word on the street was that the trigger-man was a son of one of Tiger's rivals.

"Mi bwoy. I and I can't get close to the bwoy. That's where you come into play. Star, mi ah give you tree kilos to kill dis youth." Tiger stated coldly. *"Man Tiger, just say the word. I got you. I'll do for you because I know you would do for me. Your family is my family, and your enemy is my enemy. I'll merc his whole family if you want me to,"* I told him.

I was hyped, and right about now, yo' boy was feelin' himself. *"Calm down, Star, big things ah gwan. Mi got everything in line and ready for you."* Tiger went on to let me know that the work was already back in the States and ready for me.

He also assured me that I'd be on a flight back to the U.S. as soon as the hit was completed. *"Damn,"* I thought to myself, *"Tiger needs me right now and he's willing to pass me three bricks for something I'd do for free because I fuck with him like that."*

Tiger then showed me a picture of a young cat, probably around my age. We went over everything about the mission. All the specifics from A to Z and especially about what to do once the job was done.

- - -

I was driven to a Caribbean deli and got out around the corner. The play was for me to act like I was sweeping up the general vicinity. A hittin' ass motorcycle pulled up with a bad bitch on the back. I moved in closer, confirmed that the guy riding the bike was my vic., and as soon as shorty hopped off the back and took her fine ass into the store, I moved in.

I gripped my two 45 Magnums and was up on the nigga before he could even begin to decipher what the hell was going down.

BLOCKA! BLOCKA! BLOCKA!

I pumped three hollow points into his dome, making sure that his funeral would be a closed-casket affair. Standing over him, watching his last few thoughts ooze onto the pavement, I figured I'd put two more in his chest for good measure. Wasn't no doctor in the world gonna wake his bitch-ass up. Ever!

"King! Come, star! Let's get outta here!" I heard somebody scream and a car pulled up, the back door flew open and I threw myself inside. A few minutes later, I was dropped at a second car and switched my clothes and ditched the guns.

Thirty minutes after that, I was back at the airport and, an hour past that, I was in a first-class window seat on a flight back home. As the plane climbed out into a clear, blue sky, I did my best not to think and to blank the whole, crazy trip outta my head.

Chapter Eight

So now I'm back home! My trip to Jamaica was a wild one, and I had a lot on my mind concerning the past few days. All I wanted to do was lay-up and rest my mind and soul. When I got home last night, my girls were in bed and sleeping like two beautiful babies. I decided not to wake either of them, and called it a night on the living room couch.

When I awoke the next morning, I looked around to see my things still laying around on the floor, unpacked. My phone vibrated in my pocket and caught my attention. *"Rude Bwoy. Soccer game. Gramby Street, in one hour."* Tiger said quickly. He hung up before I could even respond.

I tried calling Meth a couple of times, but to no avail so I hit God up. *"God, what's poppin' out there?"* I asked, pretending I was still in Jamaica. *"Damn, my nigga! What them thick-ass Island broads lookin' like over there?"*

That's my boy, God, nothing but hoes on his mind! *"Kik, I'm back home, nigga. Where the fuck Meth at? I been hittin' his phone with no luck, and I need you to make a quick run with me,"* I said. *"I ain't heard from him today either. We were together late last night on the block, though."* God responded. *"Yo, come see me, God."*

I got my things and hopped into the shower to try and freshen up. I let the hot water cleanse away my sins and took some time to try and clear my mind. I've been involved in a heap of nonsense these past few weeks.

I finished showering, got dressed and walked into the bedroom, where my two angels were still passed out. I planted a kiss on Sky's lips and then one on Skyla's fat cheeks. Sky woke up and flashed a *"welcome back"* smile at me. I whispered to her that I was heading out and that I would be back shortly. Sky poked her lips out for another kiss. I obliged, and left her to go back to sleep.

I stepped out of the crib feeling good about being back home. Walking down the steps, I adjusted my fitted cap down and to the left, as always. The outfit I was wearing gave me that *"money"* look. I had on a pair of buttas, complimented by thousands of dollars' worth of diamonds and gold spread out on my neck, my wrists and in my mouth.

I was a thousandaire and, most certainly, a household name in Hartford. Edgewood Street wasn't Southside Jamaica Queens, Baisley Projects, and I wasn't Kenneth McGriff, nor was my crew the Supreme Team. I was King, and my crew was them niggas from Da Woodz. We were putting in work and getting decent money, if you know what I mean.

Moosey and Meth were exiting her crib when I got to the side-walk and looked up the street. *"Kik, you back already, huh?"* he asked, giving me dap. *"Yeah, I got back in last night. Shit's official over there, Kik. We gon' have to take a trip, maybe bring the wives on vacation or something. "* I said. *"That's what's up, kik. Glad you back."*

"Damn, king, you ain't gonna acknowledge a bitch, or what?" Moosey inquired. *"Nah. it ain't even like that. You my homegirl,"* I responded. *"Well, you need to act like it then,"* she said.

- - -

When God finally pulled up, he was pushing a rental Escalade. I and Meth hopped in and we all made our way to Gramby Street. When we got to the park, shit was packed and there was a big game going on. I was in awe when I saw my Pops on the field, playing.

It's been ages since I've seen my father in action. In his younger days, he was one of the best ballers in all of Hartford, a real star. Music was playing, and everyone was smoking weed. Searching for a place to park, I saw one of Tiger's associates, rolled down my window, and hollered to him. *"King! Come through,"* he said, waving us over. *"What's up, big man?"* I asked. *"Take a lickle stroll with me, Star,"* he said, *"The I send you a gift from Yard."*

We walked together until we came to a gold-trimmed Maxima. I already knew it was that work, but Meth and God ain't have a clue about what was going on. He opened the trunk, dug in, and pulled out a bag containing the three bricks that Tiger'd promised me.

As I clutched the bag in my hands, I had a flashback of when I hit dude with those first three dome shots. *"King, the Don send 'nuff respect and say tell you him thankful for your assistance,"* he said.

Them niggas questioned me about what was in the bag. When I told them what it was, they asked what the hell I did over there that would make my connect wanna gift me three bricks, just off the strength.

I gave them a quick and dirty rundown about what had happened and let them know that the only reason that I was sharing this information is because I trusted them with my life. Them niggas respected my G, and that conversation was done, never again to be mentioned.

- - -

God dropped me off at the crib and he and Meth took it to the block, chasin' that paper. Sky's car was parked in the backyard, so I knew her and Skyla were home. Entering through the front door, I could smell something good cooking. I placed the bag of work in the bedroom closet and followed the aroma to the kitchen.

Sky was at the stove in some short-shorts and a white tank top, looking sexy and whipping up brunch. *"Damn, ma. Who you lookin' so good for? Me?"* I asked, creeping up behind her. My dick got rock-hard once it made contact with her soft ass. Ain't had no pussy in three days, so you know yo' man was dyin' for her goodies!

"Boy, don't start nothin' you can't finish. Skyla's in her room," she said. I fell back, knowing she was right. When I went to see my daughter, she was playing video games. She was so caught up in what she was doing that she did not even hear me sneak up on her.

"Boo!" I said, and she jumped. *"Hey, princess."*

"Daddy! You scared me. Wanna play Miss Pac-Man with me?"

"Yes. We can play for a little while, until mommy finishes cooking," I told her. I and Skyla played Miss Pac-Man for about an hour and a half, until Sky came to the door and demanded that we come eat. Skyla beat me three games to two.

"Daddy, you let me beat you, huh?"

"Nah, baby girl! You won fair and square," I said. No bull- shit, she was actually pretty good at playing video games. With the much time that she spends on her computer, she should be.

"Mommy, can I say grace?"

"Of course, sweetie. Go ahead," Sky told her. *"Okay! Dear Lord, thank you for blessing me with mommy and daddy. And thank you for blessing us with this food we about to eat, amen,"* she said solemnly.*"Skyla, that was lovely, my dear. You*

said grace better than daddy." Sky applauded and glanced over at me, blushing.

We finished eating and decided to watch a movie. Skyla made popcorn while Sky put in a Tyler Perry flick. We enjoyed ourselves, watching Madea cut the fool the whole damn movie. Skyla laughed herself straight to sleep and when the movie ended; I carried Skyla to her room, where she slept away the next two hours.

Me and Sky made good use of our alone time, too. She was fixing her hair in our bedroom mirror when I slid up behind her, horny as fuck, and desperately needing to be balls deep in my woman.

"Damn, ma. That ass looks like it's gettin' fatter!" She smirked and finished tying her hair up in a bun. *"Kika, I'm dead ass. You see all this?"* I asked, cupping her ass cheeks with both hands. I walked her up until she was in front of the bed then eased down her shorts, exposing her red G-string.

I slid up in her tight, juicy pussy with my middle finger soaking wet. *"Baby, you wet for daddy, huh?"* I asked. *"Yes I am,"* she replied, reaching back for my manhood. She spread her cheeks and guided my dick into her love tunnel. I started off slow, but with each thrust, the rhythm of the sex increased in tempo.

"Yeah ...Yes ...Right there," she purred.

"You want it right there, huh?"

"Yeah ..."

The head of my dick hit her walls, causing her to shudder. Her inner thigh muscles contracted around my hardness. I long-stroked that pussy as I held her waist tightly. The pounding I gave wifey had her squirting like a fire hydrant.

"Damn!" was all I could say, as I shot my nut into her pussy and collapsed on her back. Drained and fucked out, the soft kisses I placed on her upper back were music to both our ears as we fell off to sleep.

Chapter Nine

The sound of a phone ringing startled me out of my slumber.

"Yo, who this?" I answered.

"King, this Cutty. Kik, me and Forty tryna fall through."

"Just gettin' outta bed now. Gimme thirty minutes, and meet me at the Blue house," I told him.

Forty-five minutes late, I, Forty, and Cutty were at the spot handling business. Them niggas ordered two big eighths for which I charged them twenty-five hundred a piece. Cutty pulled out ten-g's and tossed me five stacks. I thumbed the pile of money, satisfied that it was all there.

- - -

Calls from all-over were coming through – The Beat, Middle Town, and New Britain. Everything was playing out, the money was flowing swiftly. God was doing well; his spots on Sterling Street and "OT" were pumping.

The Shell was doing what it does. Me and Prince were chopping it up, chillin' on the block. I respected Bro and his hustle because he was on top of his game. He wasn't out here still wildin' out like the rest of the niggas out here. He did a couple of bids but, for the most part, they were eye openers.

There were a few more homies out and about on the block at the moment, every one of them just tryna make a living. I was always preaching to them, telling them that they needed to start making all of these hustling that they were doing count for something. Niggas wasn't gonna be able to be out here doin' this shit forever.

Just like when the Old Heads were out here and we were all primed and ready to take their spots. Young cats like Lil' Mac, L-Boogie, Lil' Dee-Dee, and Lil' Hoova were ready to take our spots.

I mean, the young niggas were already out here, doing them in the 'hood. I was more than ready to pass the torch because I know how this shit goes. I lived this life twice and, from H.P. to Da Beat, I've seen it all. Believe me!

- - -

It was just past 2:30pm when I called Sky at the crib to let her know that I was on my way to scoop up Skyla. I made plans for me and my daughter to hang out and do some shopping. About an hour later, I was being dragged into Toys R Us, where Skyla was choosing all kinds of play items: from the latest, most sophisticated toys, to the newest video games on the market.

After Skyla had finished mopping the place, I had to trick her out of the store so that we could go clothes shopping. She knew there was no limit to what she could get, so she loved it when we went out to shop. Her mom only allowed her to get what she

65

believed she needed, not what she wanted. Not me, I was all about spoiling my little princess.

Trying to keep pace with Skyla was exhausting, and all the walking had made me hungry, so we hit the food court and grabbed some Mickey-D's. I don't know how she kept those little legs of hers moving all day.

After spending some quality time with my daughter, I knew she was ready to get home and play with all of her new toys and gadgets and I was ready to once again hit the streets. On the way home, a call came through I definitely wasn't up for taking. *"Yo King, it's Meth."*

"Yeah? What's the deal with you?" I asked. I could hear some tension in my man's voice. *"King, niggas came through and killed Lil' Ty. lil' Dee-Dee got hit twice too, and he's in bad shape. He's in the hospital. Man, they caught niggas slippin'. A few heads were posted up shootin' dice. Two cars hit the block, and when they got close enough, windows rolled down, guns came out, shit got ugly,"* he concluded.

I couldn't even respond to that shit; they were just kids. Ty was my little nigga; he looked up to me more than anyone in the world. *"Kik, we got word it was them niggas that came through,"* Meth said. *"Where God at? Was he out there, too?"* I asked, concerned about God's whereabouts. *"Yo, he wasn't out there. I hit his phone, but ain't got no answer,"* Meth said. *"I'm on my way. I got my little girl with me, so I'ma drop her off at my mom's crib,"* I told him.

- - -

The shit was gettin' outta hand. Lil Ty was only fourteen. Kid wasn't even hustling in the streets. How the hell were we gonna explain this shit to his parents? Later, on the block, I reached Da Woodz and saw yellow crime-scene tape hanging everywhere. You couldn't even turn on to the street, because police cruisers had the whole block shut down.

Meth hit my phone to tell me to meet him at the Shell station. People were deep at the Shell, like it was a party or something going on. *"Meth, how niggas slippin' like that, Kik?"* I asked as soon as I hopped out of the whip. *"King, I don't know. I just don't. Shit happened so fast,"* he replied. *"Damn, Meth, my little nigga gone."*

"Kik, Lil' Dee-Dee at Hartford Hospital. He got hit in his leg and arm. They hit Ty all up in his head," Meth stated. Shit was getting a bit too heavy for my heart. I had to go and calm my nerves and ease my mind a little. *"Meth, it's too hot out here for me. I'm about to take it in for the night,"* I told him.

"Aight! I'ma holler at you in the a.m. I'ma chill out here on the Deuce with niggas."

67

"Keep yo eyes open and stay on point. You strapped?"

"You already know it." We dapped each other up and I went to the crib.

- - -

I entered the house, not wanting to bother Sky. I went into the living room, opened up a window, and fired up a Haze-filled blunt. I sat back and tried to watch a few highlights on Sports Center, but I couldn't concentrate on anything but what had happened the past few weeks. First, there was the shit at Doe's party, the shootings on Tower Avenue, my Jamaica trip, and now this.

Shit was gonna have to change because getting money and beefing in the 'hood don't go hand in hand. Niggas dying over a bunch of bullshit; the Feds everywhere, and they ain't playin' no games when they handin' out football numbers for prison sentences.

- - -

The next morning, the block was filled with family and friends. We were mourning the loss of Lil' Ty. God was talking to L-Boogie and Lil' Mac when I came outside. It could've easily been any of the young soldiers. Not seeing Lil' Homies another day showed me just how short life was. I couldn't imagine losing God, Meth or a family member.

"God, what's good?" I asked.

68

"Man, kik, same shit. Just another day. This shit is crazy; homie's mom is goin' through a lot of pain losing her youngest son to these streets."

"I feel you, Kik," I stated, *"We gon' go through it with her. Niggas gonna take care of everything for his burial, and put some money up for the family."*

I headed up the street to Moosey's crib, where she and Meth were outside with her kids. *"Meth, what's poppin'?"*

"Out here, great. Just fuckin' with Moosey and the girls. Ty's death touched a lot of people," Meth said, sounding a little down.

"Meth these past few weeks have been crazy. Today we mourn the life of a fourteen-year old kid. This shit helps me make up my mind about leaving the game. When is enough ever gonna be enough?"

"King, you always told me that you got to know when the time is right. We gotta stick to the goals we set for ourselves and our families. You almost there, Kik. Basketball and school is still there for you. Everyone has their own calling. You got to decide what you gonna do."

My nigga Meth kicked some real shit, and he was dead on point with what he said. We gotta know when to call it quits. *"Damn, Moosey, you lookin' good today,"* I said. *"Yeah, okay, nigga. You gon' have Sky fuck you up,"* Moosey replied with a devilish grin. *"Girl! you know what I mean,"* I told her.

"King, I'm just playin' with you. You know we fam. Oh, by the way, my brother Shyne told me to give you his number. He said to call him sooner than later. It's urgent," Moosey said. *"Alright, tell him I'ma hit his cell later on."*

- - -

The rest of the day went by rather smoothly. I spent time on the block with Sky and Skyla. Skyla played with the other kids. She was having fun and Melony had her two daughters, so you know they raised hell.

Sky and I talked about options for finding a new house somewhere far away from the 'hood. Just watching Skyla run around on the block made me want to take them away from all the madness.

Later on that night, I finally made it around to taking a few orders. I also got the chance to call Shyne and see what he was getting into. Circling in the Acura, I punched in his number. He picked up on the third ring.

"Yo, this Shyne, who this?"

"Shyne, this yo' boy, King. How you? Moosey said you was tryna get at me."

"King, shit good on my end. I've been tryna get you for a few days now. Finally, yo' boy got at Moosey and she said she could give you my hitter. Yo, I'm speakin' for a mutual friend of

ours. He from the projects, Kik. My man wants you to know that the shit both 'hoods goin' through ain't what it looks like."

"Oh yeah? I really ain't seein' where you goin', because them project niggas are the ones behind the shootings," I said getting straight to the point. *"King, I got wind of what was goin' on, and I went to speak to my people on that end. My man said it's the youngin's behind the shootings. The old heads ain't with any of it. They wanna dead this shit before any more lives are lost,"* he said.

"Man, this shit's already outta hand," I replied. *"Well, that's why I got at you. Niggas tryna have a sit-down. You got my word that shit good on this end. I'ma hold you down, however you want me to handle it,"* he said. He told me the kid's name was Trevor from the projects.

Trev and I knew of each other from dealing with some of the same people in the dope game. I told Shyne I had to holla at niggas from around the way, but if Trevor was 100%, I was with it. *"Kik, I'ma get at you in a couple of hours with what it is with my peeps,"* I said. I hung up and got Meth and God to see what they thought about this situation.

Afterwards, we all got up with homies from Da Woodz, the Deuce, Sterling Street, Lenox, the Yard, the Jungle, East Raymond, and Enfield Street. We made sure everyone knew what was up, because we were all tied to this shit in some kind of way.

There were some mixed emotions: some were with it, others were skeptical about things. Bottom line was, we all wanted to squash the beef, but niggas didn't really trust them grimy-ass niggas.

We decided that me, Meth and Cutty would meet up and holla at Trev and his peoples. When I called Shyne back, we agreed to meet up at Bushnell Park at 10 a.m. the next morning.

Chapter Ten

It was 7 a.m. and I still hadn't been to sleep yet. I spent the night bustin' an all-nighter with Nelly and the hommie Kat. There was plenty of money out here; mad weight sales, fiends been knocking down the Blue House's doors. I wanted so badly to take my ass in the house, but there was just too much money coming through the pass up.

Around 8:30 a.m., everyone was posted on Da Woodz and the Deuce. *"Yo, King. What time niggas heading over there?"* asked Shoota. *"I told Shyne we'd be there at ten,"* I replied. *"Yo, me and Milly gon' be close by. I ain't lettin' my niggas walk into shit without us holdin' ya down."*

Shoota and Milly would be parked down the street in half a crack, ready for the worst, but hoping for the best. My Cartier watch read half-past nine. I hit Shyne up to let him know that we were on the way.

"Shyne? This King. What's the verdict?" I asked. *"I got Trevor and his man in the whip. We headed that way right now,"* he stated. *"Alright. We'll see ya in fifteen, twenty minutes."* Me, Meth and Cutty all hopped on our dirt bikes and made it to the park in record time.

Shyne, Trev, and some other OG nigga was leaning on the hood of the car when we arrived. Hopping off the bikes, we cautiously approached what could have easily been our own suicide. I dapped Shyne and gave Trev and his man a head nod.

"Trevor, what's up with you, homie? Shyne got at me about everything. We here now, so let's nip this shit in the bud," I boldly said, showing him exactly where my side stood. *"King, I'm good. I hear you good, been hearing good things about you. Yo, but on some real shit, a few young cats were behind the shit on Tower Ave., and on Da Woodz,"* he said.

He was also hinting about some businesses, but now wasn't the time. *"Being them lil' niggas from the projects, I can assure you that they have been cancelled. My peoples ain't with the bullshit. We been there and done that,"* he concluded.

"Trevor, we can respect that. Blood's been spilled on both sides. I sense loyalty in your heart. If your end is sincere with this shit, then, I give you my word, in good faith on our end. You got our word," I said. We all shook hands in hopes of a resolution that would stop the violence.

I pulled Shyne to the side, one-on-one. *"Great, you need to get up with me. Shit poppin' on my end,"* I said to him. *"Oh yeah? Yo, I'ma hit you up later, in the a.m. Kik, you know I'm for my peoples. You my dude. We came up together,"* he said.

Everyone went their own separate ways. Back home, there was a race all the way back to the block. My CR-80 was giving Cutty's KTM and Meth's KX125 pure hell! Boarded up with pins in it, my shit rode like a 250.

- - -

Meth made the call to the homies, letting everyone know that shit was dead. I let Forty and the rest of the homies know Trevor had said that the problems were taken care of. *"King, so what happens if things don't go right?"* Shoota asked.

"Kik, both sides lost. It's part of the game, and we can't get none of it back. What we can do, is stop the bloodshed," I said with a straight face, staring into the eyes of a true soldier. *"King, I'm fucked up about Lil' Ty and I don't want to lose any more lives. Yo, this a call that we all stand by."*

Politicking with these homies made me feel more comfortable, knowing the trust and them riding with the cease fire. It made me look at dudes as more than street niggas with no hearts. Don't get me wrong, they were goons but, at the same time, they had good hearts.

- - -

The weekend was a blast. We had a block party in memory of Lil' Ty, and it was awesome. Kids from all-over attended. There were all kinds of food and games for everyone. I sponsored a basketball tournament at Keney Park which turned out huge.

It's crazy how it took a tragedy to get us black people together to enjoy ourselves. In my twenty-something years of living on this earth, I've seen a lot of shit! We had a long way to go if there would be any helping society overcome the wrath of Babylon.

- - -

The festivities were now over and a new week had begun. Shit started off real crazy. I got a call from Meth, letting me know that he and God had just gotten bagged by the Narcs. The under-covers found guns and drugs in the whip. And that wasn't even the killer part – what was worse was that they were interrogated about the bodies that had turned up outside the projects.

I had Sky call the bondsman so we could get them out before it got too late. The bondsman called back to let me know their bonds were $150,000 each. I went to the stash house and got the money required for the bonds. Two hours later, both my kikos walked out of the precinct.

"Yo, what's the deal with you two crazy niggas?"

"Kik, niggas were circling, blowin' some bud, when them faggots came outta nowhere," God said, shaking his head. *"King, I think them pigs was on us all morning,"* Meth added.

They then explained how the detectives started asking about the beef between the two 'hoods and inquiring about the bodies they found outside the store the night we went through there.

Realizing the streets were talking, we concluded it'd be best to lay low for a while, until shit blew over. In the meantime, my niggas had this case to fight.

Chapter Eleven

-Meth-

The sun was fading rapidly and dark on the bight was approaching. I was the only nigga on the block and the money was coming in like clock-work. Man, I loved it this way, even though I was supposed to be laying low after that incident with me and God catching the new cases. You know me; I live for today because nothing is promised tomorrow.

The beef with them project niggas was now dead. For how long though, who knows? I was just trying to find my swag and get my bag up. It was too much money out here and niggas was finally in a position to run shit up. The homie, King was holding me down big time. Ever since kik came home from college in Buffalo, New York, he been fucking the street up.

My time was here now. I've been bullshittin' this past year jacking off my money and acting like this beefing and constant shooting was all fun and games. I got to think big and get my shit together. That shit with lil' Ty could have easily been me. After that day, I promised myself that niggas would never catch me slippin' like that ever again.

King wants to leave the game and go legit. On some real shit, I want the same thing, but I ain't ready yet; mainly money-wise. I just can't get over the hump. It feels like every time I get my head above the waters, something always get in the way stagnating me. I got access to what I need to jump up there and get my bandz up. The work ain't the problem; I need to do what I need to, to get it right because my kids are growing up fast and deserve a better life than what I had.

That's why I gotta step my game up, it's a must. There's no way I'm tryna get caught up out here and lose my life or end up doin' football numbers in somebody's jail. I have to get my mind set on the "Big Picture".

What exactly is the "Big Picture"? Living life freely, not having to keep looking over your shoulder and thinking about who's trying to kill you or lock your ass up; and being able to be out here in the world, takin' care of my kids.

- - -

After running through the last of the work I had, I shot to my spot on the Deuce to re-up. The paper was picking up as the night rolled on, but after a few more hours of running up and down the block making hand-to-hand sales, I got tired.

I then decided to hit up Keyana, one of my P.Y.T's (Pretty Young Thing). Keyana's one bad bitch; we've been fuckin' around for a minute now. A sophomore at Central Connecticut State, shorty was hot.

She lived by herself out in Bloomfield, CT. She had her own car, house and her own paper; something that was rare for young women in this part of the world. Keyana had it going on and one thing I respect in a woman is independence. It was around 2 a.m. when I called and Keyana said that she was up studying and watching TV.

It had been at least a month since I'd had any of that good pussy. When I reached her crib she answered the door wearing nothing but a towel and a smile. Shorty was super-bad, no question, but she was also freaky.

I couldn't take my eyes off her sexy figure, and she knew, by the way I was looking at her, what I was there for. She knew that me dropping by at this hour meant one thing and one thing only, booty-call, and she was always down.

She invited me in, gave me a hug and immediately stripped me down to my boxers and tank top. I wasn't even all the way inside the house when she slid my dick out of my boxers and into her mouth. I busted in a heartbeat.

Girl had a mean-ass head game. The fuck session was even better. I hit that shit doggy-style until she was calling out my name. *"Oh Meth! ...Yes! ...Fuck me harder! ...Hit this pussy! Yes! Fuck me!"* she screamed over and over again, telling me, *"This yo pussy!"*

We ended up fucking all night long until we passed out. When I woke up, it was 8 a.m., and the sun was blaring through the bedroom window. Keyana cooked breakfast, and, me being hungry, I ate and ran. Wasn't no playin' house for this nigga!

Chapter Twelve

-My New Chick-

Forty and I stepped into the Pyramid nightclub on baller status. Nigga was bored, out circling and getting high, when I asked him if he wanted to see what bitches were out clocking. We hit the bar and bought a couple of bottles of Cristal and Remy R.S.V.P. I noticed that there was a few broads at the bar tryna see if they could get a baller to offer to buy them a drink. We paid for all our drinks then found a nice secluded spot on the wall where we got twisted off some Purple Haze and got pissy drunk.

A lot of people didn't know that I was back in CT., because I hadn't really put myself out there like that. Ever since I came home, Da Woodz was all I knew. Now the Dope Boys knew where to find me, but I had a low profile.

- - -

"Yo, Forty, fire that bud up, nigga," I insisted, ready to blow. Out of the corner of my eye, I caught this fine-ass redbone walking up with her girl crew. Girl had swag and she really drew a nigga's eye. My look alone let her know that she had my undivided attention.

She approached, but threw me for a loop when she began rappin' to my homie like I wasn't even there. *"Forty? Who ya friend with you?"* she asked my comrade. *"Who dat? That's the Big Homie. Why you wanna know?"* Forty asked, puffing on his Dutch. *"Because I'm tryna holla,"* redbone replied. *"Well, why you talkin' to me, when he right here? Yo ass walked all the way over here. What? You shook or somethin'?"* Forty joked.

Shyly, she put her bid in, *"Hi. My name's Roxy. I been seein' you around for a minute, but never got a chance to kick it with you. Yet."* Ma go straight to the point. She was putting in her bid with the kid. She asked if I dance and I told her I don't dance but that I got a lil' two stepping in me. Roxy got me to the dance floor for a few songs. She was throwing her fat ass all on me, getting my shit rock hard.

Though I'm not known to be a dancer, this shawty was a beast. *"Where you from, King?"* she asked, blushing and looking sexy as ever. *"I'm from the City, but I moved to Detroit to attend school in the early nineties. I been back for a minute, but a nigga be on the low,"* I said.

We kicked it for a little while, made small talk and then she headed back to the table where her bitch-brigade was posted up. I asked Forty who shorty was and what she was about. The first thing that came to mind was that, if she wasn't no jump-off, if she wasn't out there like that, then I wouldn't mind fucking her.

- - -

Two weeks later, after a long day on the block getting that gwap, I gave Roxy a call. For the past two weeks, we'd been kicking it on the phone, and I learned a lot about her. She was actually my type, even reminded me of someone from my past – The past had me twisted.

Anyway, we rented a room at the Hilton for the night and went swimming and played in the jacuzzi. Roxy set it out when she came out of the locker room. She had on this bad ass bathing suit that showed off every curve of her body. That ass was something to die for!

We played around in the jacuzzi, splashing water on each other, just having some fun. She kept throwing her ass up on me. I got tired of all the teasing and took her up to my suite. I had the place laced with flowers, candles, fruits, and some expensive wine while listening to "The Quiet Storm."

As Roxy pulled off that little bit of clothing she had on, my manhood jumped to attention. I caressed every part of her body, from head to toe. Moaning erotically, she was on me like a wildcat in heat, pulling off my boxers and diving straight for my prized possession, taking me into the warmth of her mouth.

"Goddamn!" I hissed. Roxy's head game was on one – thousand, causing me to shoot lemonade down her throat. I knew she was a pro when she didn't let a drop go to waste. I sucked on her juicy melons, which turned her on more and more.

Laying on my back now, I was tensed as she slid her pussy lips down on me, devouring the eight inches that I was working with. *"King, I feel it ...You all up in my stomach,"* she moaned. She continued working her hips.

Not ready to bust a nut, I bent her over, face down, ass up in the air and beat her pussy up. She was grabbing the sheets and pillows – anything she could get her hands on. I gave Roxy what she wanted and she returned the favor by puttin' that pussy on a nigga!

After we sexed for what seemed like hours, we showered and ordered a late meal. We watched some television, and just kicked it. Roxy was a down to earth ass chick. She said she was single, with two kids, a son and a daughter.

I told her about Sky and my daughter Skyla, which, she said, she already knew about. We caught a few hours' sleep and woke up about 5 a.m. so that I could drop her off at home before her kids woke up.

- - -

The morning after my night with Roxy, I found myself out early chasin' that paper. That morning rush was always good, because there was never too many ma'fuckas out and about. I bumped into Forty and Cutty at Silvio's. They were in Cutty's RX-7.

Them niggas talked me into a much needed get high session. We parked on Cabot Street and they jumped into my

84

Acura. Forty and Cutty rolled up the three bags of fruits. We'd switched to my car, because there wasn't no way in hell I was tryna be with Cutty in the RX knowin' his crazy ass stay on some shit! No telling what the nigga been on, and I wasn't tryna find out.

We burned like six bags of fruits. High as a kite, we bent corners just peeping out what was poppin' in the hood. After a while, I got tired of riding around so I dropped them niggas off at Cutty's RX-7 on the Deuce. I headed 'round the corner to Edgewood Street to get some money. Prince and Solid were on the block when I pulled up and they had customers coming through in packs.

I'd only been out here for 15-20 minutes when a car came screeching around the corner and all hell broke loose. Police seemed to come from everywhere, squad cars and unmarked vehicles. They snatched up the three of us, along with a few customers who got caught lingering.

There wasn't even enough time for me to get ghost and run, being that Rodriguez and his faggot-ass side kick, Billy the Kid had guns in my face. Them two pussies threw me face down on the pavement and damn near busted my face open.

In minutes, we were all in the paddy wagon and headed down to Central Booking. Shiest had pulled up the block and through the cover of his limo tints; the cops couldn't see anyone in the truck.

– At The Station –

After sitting in the bullpen for a couple of hours, an officer came and ushered me into an interrogation room. Two detectives came in and started to question me about some of the gunplay that's been going down on the north end of Hartford.

"Well, well, Mr. Thomas, or should we call you King? The streets are talking, and your name is coming up as the answer to a lot of our questions," said the tall cop.

"I dunno what the fuck ya talkin' about, and, like you just said, the streets are talkin'. Talkin' a bunch of bullshit!" I shot back. "Is that right?" he questioned.

"And what about the reliable witnesses we got ready to nail your black ass to a cross? There's been numerous shootings in and around the city, so save the tough-guy shit for the beat cops!" The pussy-ass cops were trying to push my buttons.

"Like I said, I don't know Shit. That shoot-'em-up-bang-bang type shit ain't my specialty." Top-cop hopped out of his seat and raced around the table to get himself all up in my grill. I must've really pissed him off, because the questioning started to get physical.

"You're tough, huh? Think you're bigger than the fuckin' law? Bet you won't be tough when you're up-state doin' twenty-five to life!" Officer Dick shouted in my face, tryna scare me. These pigs know they ain't got shit on me.

We went back and forth for about an hour. The same shit, over and over again, until they finally realized they weren't gonna get shit out of me, so they hauled my black ass back to the bullpen.

"Oh yeah. Mr. Thomas? Just to let you know, you are being investigated in a multi-count drug conspiracy; you and your two friends, Meth Wallace and God Artis."

He shook me up a little bit with that piece of info. Why would they tell me if I was under investigation? Sitting in the cold and cramped bullpen, my mind was starting to race. I was tryna figure out who might be working with the police, because they sure seemed to know a lot about me and my people.

The turn-key finally made it around to give me my one phone call, and I used it to call Sky. She said she'd be on her way to bail me out.

I've been a little skeptical about a lot of things that'd been going on in these streets.

The last few times the block was hit; it couldn't be just a coincidence that certain niggas weren't around. Could it? I needed to holla at God and Meth about this shaky-ass shit, so we could keep our eyes open and weed out the snake in the grass.

Chapter Thirteen

-Court's in Session-

I woke up in the comfort of my own bed. I had court this morning on the drug charges that stemmed from the arrest on the block. I knew the charges were bogus, and that had me feeling pretty good about the whole situation.

I picked up my brother, Nelly, from Queen's house so we could be in court by 8 a.m. My lawyer, Mr. Guiliano, was waiting on me at the front entrance when we arrived. We were able to get a quick, fifteen minutes meeting in, before our case came up on the docket.

The Bailiff had everyone stand when the Judge entered the courtroom. As the Judge sat and banged his gavel, he ordered the entire room to be seated. He then read the docket sheet, and called our case first.

The charges were read and the Prosecutor presented his case. We were being charged with numerous drug counts and some other minor charges. It was a preliminary hearing, and the State was trying to revoke our bonds.

Mr. Guiliano whispered to me that the Prosecutor was simply trying his hand; he promised that we were going to be good. *"Your Honor, the Defendants are charged with numerous felony drug crimes and we are close to bringing down assault and murder charges as well,"* the Prosecutor stated.

"Objection! Your Honor, there are no murder charges on this indictment, so the State is out of bounds with any accusations claiming differently," Guiliano nearly screamed with fury.

"Counsel? Will the State please refrain from making allegations, and please stick to the charges being filed, the charges at hand?" the Judge ordered, eyeing the Prosecutor's table sternly.

"But Your Honor, the murder charges are being sought as we speak." The Judge wasn't hearing any of it. He told the Prosecutor that now wasn't the time. He then issued his Ruling.

"In light of the State's case, I know that these are some serious felonies, but at this time, the defendants are not being heard on murder charges, that being said, I see no reason to revoke their bonds. This case is in its early stages, and if things were to change for the worse, then I will deal with it accordingly at that time. This case is set to continue next month, on the 25th. Court is now adjourned, have a nice day." He banged his gavel again and called the next case.

Outside in the car, I hit Meth's cell-phone. He was at the Blue House, smoking bud and playing X-Box. *"Kik, what's up, my boy?"* I asked.

"I'm good, King. Just in the spot, doing me. I just heard how shit played out in court. I'm glad the Judge played fair."

"*Great, they talkin' about murder charges on the way. My lawyer said they got people talking, but he doesn't know who and how much.*"

I also let him know that I wasn't comfortable at all, out there on the block or even layin' my head anywhere in the 'hood. Not only, was the, law tryna take us down, one of our own people was working for them. My new motto was, "*outta sight, outta mind.*" The less niggas knew and saw, the better!

Chapter Fourteen

-God-

Just when the going gets good and the money starts pouring in, here come the fuckin' haters. Meth, King and I are eating lovely out here. We are reaping the benefits of all the good work that King is getting from Tiger.

Ever since Meth and I caught them charges in my whip, shit been ugly. We've been playing things safe. We ended up getting probation for those charges, but this new shit they puttin' together on us is crazy.

The ballgame is being played the wrong way. There ain't no telling what we're up against. I've been pulling the graveyard shift lately. Those were the only hours that seemed safe. I catch weight sales here and there, but this shit was unheard of around the way. Niggas ratting at an all-time high.

Cruising down the Avenue, I was wondering what my next move was gonna be. I spotted Meth turning off Kent Street, and I flagged him down and we both turned into the carwash. He was most likely coming from seeing Briggs and Nephew.

"Great, what's up with you?"

"Shit, you know me. Hittin' Briggs and them up for that Haze. What's up with you?"

"Shit. I was just bendin' corners out here, gettin' it, Kik, Yo boy was just in the whip, thinkin' about what's been goin' on these past few months. The old case, now this new shit hangin' over our heads," I said. *"Man, we gotta tighten up our circle, and do it in a way that lets us keep gettin' this money. Shit a little shakey out here,"* Meth stated.

We politicked and blazed up the piff while two Old Heads washed the trucks. We decided to hook up and hit up Tasty's, a strip club located in East Hartford.

– Later that Night–

Tasty's was a spot that catered to all of the ballers and wanna-be ballers. Some of the baddest bitches from all-over Connecticut worked there. When I whipped to Uptown's spot, pushing my 1968 Z-28 Camaro R5; Meth was going nuts seeing my shit-mint condition, and sitting on chromes.

"Damn, Kik! When you cop this bitch?"

"A couple days ago," I told him.

"This bitch fast, she got 250 on the dash."

When my nigga got in, I threw her in first gear and was in fifth in a matter of seconds. *"God, this bitch got balls. You hurtin' 'em with this!"* I tossed Meth a quarter ounce of Haze and a box of Dutches. Taking a whiff, the fruity mixture of grapes and assorted berries hit his nostrils immediately.

On our way to the club, we must've blown three blunts, and I was twisted. A little Remy on top of the Haze had me right where I wanted to be. Stepping into Tasty's, the sight of all those beautiful women walking around, just strings from being naked, giving lap-dances and doing sets on-stage that brought me back.

Moments after we'd gotten comfortable at a table, two fine broads walked up offering dances. They were too sexy, long-legged dime pieces. I mean thick in all the right places. *"How much?"* Meth asked them both, whipping out a knot of fifties and hundreds.

Instantly, you could see the reaction in their faces. They were certainly happy to have spotted us before all the other girls. *"Twenty a song,"* the lighter of the two said. They ended up giving us a couple of songs for free.

The bitch that I ended up with had it going on – fat ass, nice sized tities, she really was put together. She was throwing her goodies all over me and I was very much enjoying giving her my hard earned money.

Looking over at Meth, I saw the other broad whispering in his ear while dangling her tities in his face. Shortly after, they were headed to one of the VIP rooms, and I knew Meth done talked shorty into giving up the pussy.

A half-hour later, with this sweaty bitch still shakin' her ass on me, I got tired and dismissed her, wanting to see what else this spot was working with. From the looks of things, there were a few baller-type niggas in the building.

Up on stage was this sexy, short and thick chick, doing her thing on the pole. She was hanging upside down, legs wide open, and showing everyone in the place her fat-ass pussy. I got a spot up front so that I could watch her do her thing.

She hit the floor on all fours and made her ass shake like Jell-o. Niggas was throwin' bills all-over the stage. Not fazed at all, Shorty stayed focused and mesmerized everyone in attendance.

Still on all fours, she looked my way, stuck her finger inside her pussy and then sucked her own juices off. Shorty was checking me hard, like she seen something in my eyes. Nodding my head, I let her know that feelings were mutual.

When she finished her set, Shorty left the stage with bills stuck everywhere. As I was heading back to my table, I felt a soft hand touch my shoulder. I turned around and found myself staring into the most beautiful eyes I have ever seen.

"What's up, sexy?" I asked her, knowing that I was looking at the baddest bitch in the club. *"Yo', I hope you liked the show. I put a little extra into the performance when I saw you looking at me."* Shorty was tryna see how much I was diggin' her. Little did she know that digging her back out was all on my mind.

"What's on your mind, beautiful? You tryna leave with the kid, or what?" I asked, since we were both being straight forward.

"It's whatever with me, big boy. Let me get my things and we can be out. My shift's 'bout over anyways."

A few minutes later, Meth exited the V.I.P. room with his chick in tow. I let him know about Shorty, and told him that she was riding out with me tonight.

– 20 Minutes Later –

Shorty strutted towards the table looking sexier than she did on the pole. She said her name was Champagne, and I told her my name was Chris, and we all hopped into my whip. I dropped Meth off at his truck, and Shorty and I headed over to the Hilton in downtown Hartford.

Champagne hopped in the shower and I rolled up some bud. Ma came out of the bathroom with nothing on. Caramel complexion, she was fine. She approached me and started helping me out of my clothes, then proceeded to give me head.

I mean she was the truth. The girl had my head spinning like a top. I gave her a condom and she slid that shit on with her mouth. Bending her over, I hit that pussy doggy-style for a good fifteen minutes. Her pussy was so wet and tight.

"You like this tight pussy, baby?" she taunted, taking every pump like a pro. *"Chris, I'm cumming,"* she moaned. Hearing that name threw me, I'd almost forgotten that that was the name I'd given her.

"Deeper ...Go deeper. Please, I want to feel you in my belly." Shorty was a freak. She even wanted me to hit her in the ass, so I gave her what she wanted. Starting to feel I was about to nut, I pulled out, took the condom off and had her suck me dry.

Around 4 a.m., I slid my clothes back on, and placed $300 for the fuck and $50 for a cab ride home. I pushed the Camaro to the crib, took a shower, and got some sleep.

Chapter Fifteen

Finding a new house wasn't as easy as I thought. I got hooked up with this real estate company through one of my close friends. My associates helped me set up tomorrow as a day to go and check out a few houses they had on the market. My main concern was finding something, somewhere, that was a good fit for Sky and Skyla.

- - -

The next day, at 9 a.m., I was seated in my Acura waiting on who knows. I wasn't sure who they would be sending to show me the house but I didn't care as long as they could help me find a nice place for my two baby girls. I needed to get them far away from the hood and all the nonsense that was going on in Hartford.

Ten minutes later, a red, bubble-eyed Benz pulled up and out stepped one of the baddest sisters I have ever laid eyes on. *"Hello, you must be Mr. Thomas. My name is Tammy, Tammy Smith,"* she said while extending her hand for a shake. I returned the gesture and grasped her hand firmly, mirroring the confidence she was displaying.

"Hello to you, Ms. Smith, Tammy. And may I just say that you are looking mighty nice this morning," I shot back, making her blush and bringing a Kool-Aid smile to her face. We decided to take her car, so I left my whip in front of the civic center.

"*Well now, Mr. Thomas, tell me a little bit about where and what you would like your new home to be.*"

"*Honestly, I'm just looking for something respectable and comfortable enough for my two girls, nothing too flashy or extravagant.*"

Next thing I know, we were headed towards West Hartford. The first house she showed me was built like a mini-mansion; it had four bedrooms, two bathrooms and a swimming pool in the back yard. I knew instantly that Sky would fall in love with this spot. There was no need to even look at another house. I was locked in on this one.

"*Ms. Smith, this is the first and the last stop. I am sold on this one. Somebody will be by your office in the morning to take care of all the paperwork and the financials.*" I also let her know that my plans called for me to move my family in immediately.

I'd keep the crib in Da Woodz for me, and I'll give Sky a healthy budget to furnish our new home. You know how women get with money and shopping.

- - -

Two days later, my brother Max hit my phone to let me know that the deal for the house was finalized. He had the lawyer take care of the insurance part. After picking up the keys, I headed home to pick up Sky and Skyla.

When we arrived in front of the big house, they both asked me who lived there. *"My family lives here,"* I said, at the same time as I passed the keys to Sky. The look in her eyes was worth a million words. Walking through the back gates and up to the oak door, I could tell they were both excited, and that I'd made the right choice.

Sky inserted the key and opened the door and her and Skyla both jumped on me, hugging and kissing me repeatedly.

"King, it's so beautiful!"

"Just like you, Sky," I kissed her.

"I knew you'd love it, that's why I bought it for you. For us. It was time I moved you two out of the 'hood. I want to raise Skyla in a better, safer environment." Skyla had already run off to sight-see. *"Daddy, which one of these rooms is mine?"* Skyla asked. *"Anyone you want besides the master, baby girl. That one is for me and mommy."*

Sky was talking a mile a minute, telling me how she envisioned decorating every last inch of the house. She was going to have a lot of furnishing to do, given the size of our new spot. She wasted no time in getting things together so that we could move.

I spent the next couple of days helping Sky shop around and pick up all the things she had ordered and purchased for the new house, and it had me worn out. She was working the hell out of me! She had the movers deliver everything and place them where she wanted them.

She figured it would be smart for me to be present when the movers showed up, it'd be a good idea to have a man around. There's no telling who you might find yourself dealing with these days. After the deliverymen finished and left, I let Sky know that I had to get out of the house for a while, and that I would be back later.

On my ride to the 'hood, I received a call from Meth telling me that him and God needed to see me. I took a guess on what they needed to see me about and let him know that I'd meet them at the Blue House. When I got there, my two men were inside and waiting on me.

I let them know how things were turning out with the move into my new spot. I had to admit, moving the wife and daughter away from all of this madness was one hell of a stress reliever. The 'hood wasn't a good place to raise a family, especially when a nigga like me was knee-deep in the drug game. We got high and kicked it while customers beat the Blue House's doors down.

None of us was getting anywhere with our inquiries as to who could be giving the cops their information. I let them know that my lawyer had informed me last week that the State's case was a weak one, but we still needed to stay out of the limelight.

It was easier said than done though, knowing that there was a rat loose somewhere in our circle. It was something we had to do, something in our best interest if we wanted to stay free men.

Chapter Sixteen

-King-

It's been a few months now, since we moved into the new crib. Business has been running smoothly, but for some reasons, shit's been going in the wrong direction at home with the wife. Insecurity and Sky's people getting in my business started to get on my bad side.

The fact that my loyalty was being questioned turned me off. I found myself fighting and arguing over petty shit, and that wasn't my style. Some of her girls were just doing way too much, I mean, she had some cool friends like Tela, Melony, Lashonda, and Tracy, but some of them other ducks were in the way.

Put plainly, I was getting tired of the bullshit. Sky is my heart, but I won't let anyone hold me back. I'd rather be lonely and miserable by myself. Being that ain't the route I'm tryna take though, I'm in a spot. I couldn't live without Sky and Skyla.

Late night, I hit the La Marage pool hall that all the Avenue niggas frequented. When I entered the spot, my niggas Rain, Rugged, Horse, and Yella was getting twisted and betting on their pool games. I joined the party and purchased rounds of Remy for everybody.

I ended up getting beat out of a 'hundred dollars to Rain. Underestimating his pool game, he gave me a lesson and, if I would have stayed longer, he would've taken all the cash I had on me. I left there drunk and feeling right, with lust on my mind.

I didn't want to go home, so I gave Roxy a call. She picked up on the second ring. *"Hello, may I know who's calling?"* she asked, not recognizing the number.

"It's your secret admirer. How many of those do you have? Nah. It's King."

"Hey King, I'm sorry. I didn't know the number. Glad to hear from you, what's the special occasion?"

"You were on my mind, so I thought to give you a call."

"Oh, how nice. I just put the kids to bed, and now I'm laying here and watching TV."

"Roxy, what you got planned for tomorrow?" I asked, hoping that we could spend some time together. Hanging out with her might get my mind off a lot of the bullshit.

"After I drop the kids off at school, I ain't got nothing planned."

"How about we get together for lunch? If that sounds good to you," I asked. I really wanted her company, and was praying that she'd accept my offer. She did, and we set up 12:30 p.m. That was a good time because it gave me room to go home to the West, tighten up, and also have some time to handle my morning routine with the spot.

The next morning, I was up and about my business, making some early pickups and drop offs. Everything was going smoothly. I ended up firing up a Dutch while I got ready for my lunch date with Roxy. I was going to show her the genuine, everyday side of me today. I was really feeling her, and could see her on my side, holding me down.

"Hey Roxy, it's King, I'll be pulling up any minute now."

"Okay, King. I'm just about ready. I'll be waiting on you out front."

Knowing how slow women are, I decided to bust a few corners and give her a few more minutes. When I pulled up, she was just coming out the door. I reached over and opened the passenger door for her.

I was dumbstruck with awe, looking at the beauty that was sitting beside me. Her dress was amazing; a bright and beautiful tone that complemented her skin. *"This is nice,"* she said, referring to my 1994 Azure. *"Thanks, ma. It was a gift for all of the hard work I've been putting in."*

We headed out to this fancy Italian restaurant on the East, not too far from her crib. Arriving at the spot, it was actually beautiful inside, and decorated very nicely. We ordered glasses of their best wine as our food was being cooked. Roxy was looking fine as hell! As I looked into her eyes, she looked back into mine, all I could see was a person I wouldn't mind having a future with.

My life was very crazy when it came down to women. The simple fact was that now, there were two women who had love for me. Two women that I had love for back. Each one's personality drew my love in a different way.

The waitress appeared with our meals and we talked as we ate. We laughed, we had fun, and we made the best out of our little slice of time together. Time flew rapidly, and it had grown later than we thought. Her kids would be getting out of school soon, so we finished up at the restaurant. *"King, it's getting late, and I have to pick the kids up from school."*

"If you want, I'll take you to pick them up," I offered. She thanked me, but let me know that she had a few other things to take care of with her family. *"I want to thank you and I want you to know that I had a wonderful time today."*

"You are very welcome, and I want to thank you for allowing me to show you a good time." Walking out to the car, we were hand in hand and it felt like we had been together forever. As I opened the passenger-side door, she gazed into my eyes and kissed me.

My head was spinning non-stop as I drove her home. What the hell was I thinking? This woman is perfect, but I have a wife at home who, besides her insecurities, is perfect for me. After spending the day with Roxy, I felt refreshed. Hanging out with her was fun, and I looked forward to chilling with her again.

Chapter Seventeen

-Sky-

It's been almost a week, and I've been getting the same shit from King. When he eventually comes home, which is usually late, he checks in Skyla and then goes to his so-called, "business only" room to sleep. I know he's got a lot on his plate right now, but cutting me all the way out ain't gonna help.

Last month, he found a phone number that I forgot to throw away, and it really pissed him off. I couldn't even really argue with him because I was in the wrong. We talked about it, and I told him it was nothing, but as anyone who knows him will tell you, he's not one to let shit slide just like that.

He said he wasn't tripping about it anymore, but I know he's on some bullshit. He would never stay away from his family for days at a time unless he felt like shit was really going south between us. When I called him this morning, he answered sounding groggy, like he'd just woke up.

"Baby! Where you at?"

"Sky, you know where I'm at. I'm at the other house. I was out all night drinking, so I just stayed here."

"Boy, you know I would have come and get you. Why didn't you call? Your daughter has been asking of you. What am I supposed to tell her?"

"Tell her I'll be able to get her later, so that we can catch the Connecticut Sun's Women's basketball game."

"Alright. Are you coming home soon? I want to talk about us and spend some time with my man."

"Yeah, you got that. Tell Skyla to be ready when I get there. The game starts at seven."

For the time being, I felt a little bit better. After talking to King this morning, it put me at ease to know that he would be coming home tonight, and that we'd have a chance to talk and really see what was going on with us.

After he came and picked up Skyla, I got myself together and called Tela to see if she wanted to chill for a while. She was up for hanging out, so I drove over to her crib, parked in her driveway, and headed to her front door.

"Hey girl! Come on in. What you gonna do? Stand out there all day?"

"No. I was just waitin' on yo' ass to get outta my way!"

She stepped aside and laughed at my response. I hung my coat up on her coat rack and took a seat in the living room.

"Girl, I'm so glad you came over. I've been in here bored to death. I dropped the girls off at their grandmother's house."

"King came home and got Skyla and took her to a WNBA game at the Mohegan Sun Casino and Resort. Skyla was so happy; you know she loves basketball just like her daddy."

That ain't no lie. My man loves him some ball, too. Always saying he wished he could get another shot at college. Now Skyla: It's in her blood, she loves playing. I just wish the problems King and I are having wouldn't keep him away from her.

"*What's been up with you, Sky?*"

"*Not much, Tela. Been stayin' home a lot, me and Skyla. Besides, me and King beefing.*"

"*Girl, why you two beefin' now?*"

"*He found an old phone number some nigga gave me at the club one of them nights we went out.*"

"*Sky, is you trippin'? What, you creepin?*"

"*Nah, it ain't even like that. The nigga was tryna holla. I took his digits so he'd leave me alone, and I just forgot to throw it out when I left.*"

"*Sky, I know he fucked up with you right now.*"

"*Fucked up ain't the half of it, girl. Most nights the nigga ain't even comin' home.*"

"*You think he's messin' around?*"

"*Shit, I dunno! I just know he ain't been sleepin' in my bed.*"

Tela and I chopped it up for a while until we got hungry. We contemplated going out to eat, but decided to stay in. Tela went into the kitchen and fried up some chicken and rice. We ate, and then I hurried home to get ready for King and Skyla when they got back.

108

Chapter Eighteen

-Daddy's Lil' Girl-

"Skyla, you ready to go in here and watch the big girls?"

"Yeah, Big Head, you know I'm ready. I been askin' you to take me to a game for a month now! Daddy, who the Sun playin' today?"

"They playin' the Indiana Fever, big girl. The team I told you Tamika Catchings plays for. I want you to watch her; you'll learn a lot from her."

I loved that my little girl was into basketball. I'd always wanted a son to follow in my footsteps, playing sports-wise. When Sky gave birth to Skyla, I always used to say that she'd be like me and better. Sky would always laugh and say, *"Yeah right, you see she looks like me."*

Actually, she just had her mom's complexion. From my head, ears, hands, hell, even my actions and mannerisms, we had it the same. Her liking sports, that took the cake. Daddy's lil' girl is what I always called her.

- - -

The arena was jam-packed, with the people there for the game to the ones that were there to gamble away their hard earned money, the casino was making bank! We hit the concession stand where

109

Skyla ordered a bunch of junk food, while I ordered nachos and cheese, also some drinks.

We found our seats just as the starting lineups were being announced. *"See Skyla, one day that's gonna be your name being called out. You'll be old enough to play with the big girl."* I told Skyla. The game was about to start and everyone was looking forward to a Sun victory.

When the game started, the Connecticut Sun went on a 6 – 0 in the first three minutes. Skyla was locked into what was happening, she was clapping and yelling at the Connecticut players to shoot the ball and tighten up on defense. I was happy to see my lil' girl having so much fun. She was acting like she was on the bench playing.

The game was so intense and the Sun was doing a number on the Indiana Fever; but at the beginning of the second quarter, the Fever crawled back into the game with a run of their own.

"Come on, Sun!" Skyla screamed. We were in the third row, and the stadium was loud as hell, but couldn't nobody tell my lil' girl that the players couldn't hear her. *"Skyla, you having fun?"* I asked, to which she responded *"Yes daddy. I always have fun when we're together."*

Halftime came and the Connecticut Sun was holding on to a 10 point lead; they were on their A-game tonight. This was actually my first time watching Tamika Catching play live and up close. She was the truth; I mean she played just like a boy. I can't even lie; I'd probably have a problem with her myself.

Going down to the wire, the Sun found its way to come out with a 7 point win and was able to defeat the top team in the conference. Skyla and I stayed in our seat cheering them on right up until the last second on the clock ticked off the clock.

"Thank you, daddy. I really had fun spending time with you today. When can we come back and watch another game?"

"Kika, I will let you know when the next home game will be and I'll get us some tickets. Maybe we can get mommy to come with us next time."

- - -

–Back at Home–

When Skyla and I got home and entered the house, it was smelling like a soul food spot in our crib. Skyla ran upstairs to her room, probably to play PS3. I went straight to the kitchen to see what Sky had going on there.

I found Sky whipping some chicken wings, macaroni and some corn on the cob. *"Hey ma, what you got cooking in here?"* I asked. I planted a soft kiss on her neck and told her I miss her crazy ass.

"Oh, just puttin' a little something together for my King and my little princess."

"*That's good, because I'm starving for some real food. Your little princess had me eating junk food all day. Here she comes now.*" I said as Skyla came running her bad-butt down the stairs.

"*Mommy, Mommy! We went to the Mohegan Sun and watched the Connecticut Sun play against the Indiana Fever in the basketball game! Daddy wants me to be like Tamika Catching, but I want to play like Maya Moore, she is the best.*"

"*Princess, I didn't know you even knew who Maya Moore was.*"

"*Daddy, I watch girls' basketball on TV all the time! You just never home to see me.*"

That was a shot to the gut, but she was right. I was spending too much time in the streets and not enough time at home with my family. When the food was finally finished, we sat down and said the grace before eating our dinner. Sky actually did her thing and the food was the bomb! I ain't tasted her food and had it taste that good in a long time!

It was around 9 p.m. when we finished eating. It was almost Skyla's bedtime, so she went upstairs to take a bath and probably sneak in a video game or two before her bedtime actually rolled around.

Sky cleaned up and I took the trash out to the dumpster and went up to take a shower. Five minutes in, Sky had joined me.

We washed each other clean and kicked it about what was going through both of our minds.

"King, what's really goin' on with us? Shit ain't the same."

"Kik, I don't really know. There's a lot of things going on in my life right now. Dealing with these streets, dealing with this case, it's all tearing me up."

"But why ain't you comin' home? Skyla and I need you here with us."

"Sky, you already know the answer to that shit."

"Bae! I told you that phone number ain't nothing! You still don't believe me?"

"It ain't about do I or don't I. The thing is, you my queen. You ain't supposed to let no nigga feel he can get next to you. These niggas out here know what it is with me. If they can get some rap from you, they gon' feel like shit can go further, and I ain't down for that shit."

"I see your point, and I promise, it ain't gonna happen again." We talked some more, laid up in bed, hugged up like a teenage couple.

Chapter Nineteen

I was parked up the block in the Acura, just chilling, when Guiliano, my lawyer, called with some really good news.

"Good morning, Mr. Thomas. How are you?"

"I'm doing fine, Mr. Guiliano, how about yourself?"

"Fine, fine. I have some info that's going to make your day," he said with a chuckle, *"the State of Connecticut will no longer be pursuing the murder charges, and the pending drug case has been dropped due to lack of evidence."*

"Man! You ain't bullshitting me, are you?"

"Not at all, Mr. Thomas. I would never play with something so serious. I will tell you this though; don't think, not even for a minute, that the law is not going to be watching you and your boys. We dodged a bullet here, but they'll still be gunning for you, trying to build other cases."

"I know. Look, Mr. Guiliano, I appreciate you and everything you've done. I knew I hired the right lawyer."

"You are very welcome, King. I am glad it all worked out. Be more careful, but call me if you need me."

After the phone call with my lawyer, I popped in Mobb Deep's "Infamy" CD and leaned the driver's seat all the way back, dirty low. I rolled a Dutch of that fire-ass Haze and thought about the rest of the work I had stashed at the spot.

It was time for me to get at Tiger and re-up; I think I got a little over half a brick left, and the way things were moving out of here, that short shit surely gonna be finished by the end of the night.

My boy JT from Dutch Point called me up trying to purchase two birds, and he was right on time. I could put my order in, get JT's money, and handle my business. In the process, I'd make ten racks off of him. A few hours later, JT and I met up and I got his money.

I left him and headed to the Sportsman's Club on Main Street. Tiger was already there waiting on me when I arrived. The exchange went smoothly and I left to meet back up with JT. He was good with the product, and we went our separate ways. I felt a lot better immediately I gave him his shit and got back around the way, where I felt safe.

– Just like the good ol' times –

I was spending more time with the family. After school, I picked Skyla up and took her to the YMCA, where she played on the girls' basketball team. Sky and I were back doing shit we used to do when we first met. Getting ready to hit the streets and make a few moves, I stepped into the bedroom to let Sky know that I was stepping out.

"King, where you headed to? I'm tryna ride out with you."
She could see it in my eyes that I wanted to say hell nah, but I

straightened my face up and invited her along. *"Aight, get ready. We on a mission."*

She didn't take long doing her "girly thing" in the mirror. We took the Benz and she drove me around while I handled my business. It reminded me of the good ol' times, back when she never left my side, not even for a second. I had three drops to make and also had to hit the Blue House and pick up the work that I had orders for.

The first person I hit was my nigga Scotty, from The Square. He hit me for a hundred grams of soft. We met up with him at the basketball court in the projects. Next, we drove to Bedrock, so I could holla at Petey at the 24-hour spot. Petey's my young nigga, a Puerto Rican ma'fucka who fucked with that Diesel, and was also known to fuck with that Girl on the side.

"Let's go, Sky. We out," I said as we set out to hit our final destination. *"Where we headed to now, big daddy?"*

"Shoot out to the field, Block and them niggas waitin' on me." Driving down Mather Street, she made the right, turning up Enfield. I told her to pull a couple of houses down from the crib where they hung at.

"Yo, Block, I'm outside, nigga!" I spat into my cell-phone. *"Come in, King. Front door's open, we all up in here on it."* I grabbed the two eights and told Sky to give me five minutes. When I walked in, the music was on blast, and these niggas was getting twisted.

116

They had a few bitches in the spot, too. Kool-Aid led me into a back-room, where Block and Pillz was counting banded stacks of money. *"Yo, Kik. We respect yo' G, and you been playin' fair for a minute now."*

"Man, you niggas know what it is. Real niggas play fair with real niggas," I said, letting them know that it was bigger than money with us, we were homies. Them niggas was like little brothers to me.

"Aight Kik, we gon' holla."

"Aight, do that. I'll be around."

– Back in the Car –

"Sky, what time is it?"

"Almost 5:15, about time to go pick up Skyla from the YMCA." I was getting hungry, and asked Sky what she was in the mood to eat. She said we'd figure it out once we picked our daughter up. I was a little uneasy at the prospect of Skyla deciding on our menu, she'd end up with us eating ice cream, or some other junk food.

Arriving in front of her program, we spotted Skyla out front talking to some of her friends. Seeing us pull up, she said her goodbyes and headed to the car. *"What's up, big-head girl?"* I asked, kissing her on the forehead.

"Nothing daddy," she replied, wiping my kiss off. She always acted embarrassed when I showed affection to her in front of her friends.

"Hi mommy!"

"Hey baby."

Skyla buckled her seatbelt and we all decided on Outback Steakhouse for dinner.

- - -

– Days Later –

With the summer coming fast, the weather was really heating up. Meth and God's pockets were getting fat, and it made me feel good to see my niggas doing their thing. Me? I was stacking heavy and talking with Tiger about other ventures on the horizon.

On the block, my brother Prince and Kat and Vee were doing big things too. Their pockets were starting to bulge. From the whips, jewelry, and bigger supply that was being paid for, everybody was doing good. Some homies were still on the bullshit, but they couldn't help it; busting guns was all that they knew.

I did my best to stay away from that type of shit unless the situation called for it. That's why the news Meth hit me with a few hours ago caught me more than a little off-guard.

– Two hours earlier –

My phone was vibrating and I'd just managed to hit "SEND" before the call disconnected.

"Yo, King, this Meth. I need you to swing by the crib. I need to rap with you on some serious shit."

"I ain't far, yo' boy was just out here circlin' blowin' on that good shit. I'm on my way," I said. I was wondering what he had on his mind that he couldn't or wouldn't talk about on the phone. I got to his spot and rolled a Dutch while I waited. It didn't take long. *"Pass that shit, nigga,"* said Meth as he dropped into the passenger seat next to me.

"Slow down, nigga, that's a killa."

"Everything's a killa to you, Kiko, you smoke too much." He hit the blunt twice and broke into a choking fit. *"Damn, Kik!"* he said between coughs, *"where you get this shit from?"*

"Nigga, I told you, I only fuck with that killa. See, yo' ass 'bout to O.D. right here in the whip!"

I pulled off and drove around the city, puffing on piff. *"Meth, what was you tryna holla at me about?"* I was anxious to know what was on his mind. *"I dunno if you been 'round the way yet, homie, but Robb and a couple of his men got stuck up on the block last night."*

Meth went on to say that his brother Rocky said the niggas even asked about if they knew who King was. Whoever them cats were, they had balls. They came through hard body. Meth said Rocky told him the niggas weren't even wearing ski masks.

119

Meth made a few calls around to see if anyone heard anything. One thing's for sure, soon enough the streets would start talking, and when they do? We'd be listening.

- - -

Two days of lookin' into who was behind the stickups on the block, something finally panned out. One of Meth's associates on South End came to us with some niggas he heard had hit a lick around our way. Some nigga named Chucky was behind it all. He ran with some old-heads, old-timer cats that used to get money. Looking for a big score, my name must have come up. I knew these mafuckas didn't know me though, let alone what I looked like.

God, Meth and I got up with Meth's peoples and came up with a plan to get at Chucky. Them niggas was gonna holla at Chucky and let him know that they had a major lick lined up. Also, they were looking for an outsider to get involved, because the people getting hit knew them.

– Days later, on the South End –

Chase hipped Chucky to what seemed like a no-brainer. Without thinking twice, Chucky jumped at the thought of a come-up. *"What type of figure we talkin' about?"* asked Chucky, rubbing his hands together greedily.

"A few hundred G's. If you got one trustworthy nigga, we can use him. We gonna split everything fifty-fifty."

"That's what's up, Chase. We in. When we makin' the move?

"Shit set up for tomorrow. You gonna be ready?"

"Yeah, count me in."

Little did Chucky know that Chase and his team were collecting their cut, and him and his partner were meetin' their maker for fuckin' with the wrong niggas.

The next night, Chucky and one of his men showed up at the house, ready to put in some work. Neither him nor his man knew who they were dealing with, sitting in the same spot as the people they were sticking! These two ducks were clueless.

Chase sent Meth and God to the back for the guns we'd be using. Chucky got all hyped up, seeing the artillery. *"Yo, these niggas we 'bout to hit be gettin' that bread,"* I said, pouring a little gas on the fire. Chucky asked who the marks were, and where'd they lay their heads at.

"The nigga King, he from the North End, he sellin' major weight on the A.V.E."

"Yo, I know the nigga. He hustles over on Edgewood Street. I been on that nigga, this makes shit even better, 'cause I ain't know where he rested at."

Hearing that this nigga had been on me sent a shock through my veins. I looked over at Meth who was steaming, about to blow over, and I knew shit was 'bout to get ugly. *"Kik, let's get this shit poppin',"* said God, whipping out his .357. As if on cue, Meth and I followed suit, upping our own iron.

"Yo! Yo! What's up with your peoples, Chase?" Chucky mouthed. Running up on him, I pistol-whipped his bitch-ass, sending blood flying out of his mouth. *"You bitch-ass nigga! How you gon' stick a nigga you ain't ever seen?"*

"What you talkin' 'bout, young blood"

"My name ain't young blood, nigga! I'm dat nigga, King you been lookin' for!"

He stood frozen when he heard and understood what I had just said. Chucky knew shit was serious, knew that he was staring death in the eyes, and he made a quick move for the door. BOOM! -BOOM! - BOOM! - was the only sound, as slugs from Meth's .45 dug deep into his back. Simultaneously, I emptied my Glock, sending Chucky's quivering body to the ground, riddled with bullets.

We ran for the whip and handed Chase a duffel bag filled with thirty-g's. He told us that he'd handle the body, and not to worry about the mess. There wasn't a speck of remorse in our hearts, and we continued on with our lives and our business, as usual.

Chapter Twenty

-Summer Time-

It'd been a couple of months now, since we dealt with that dead stickup nigga, Chucky, and the city was talking. Word was, he'd pulled a bunch of robberies right before his demise, and rumor had it Da Woodz had been victimized by his hand.

"Did he know he was walkin' into a trap?"

"Was it King and his team?"

Those were just a few of the questions being asked. Shit was smooth on our end and we just kept doing us. There ain't no way that shit could blow back on us, so we weren't sweating it.

- - -

Summer was finally here and Hartford was known as "Baby New York City." The hot weather brought out the money, but it also brought out the haters. Everyone was tryna see who was doing what, and it wasn't just the niggas. The bitches were on it too, getting money any and every way that they could – hustling, drugs, men, even their bodies. The broads out here were vicious as any nigga in these streets.

Summer League basketball was here, and you know I stayed in shape, playing ball whenever I got the chance. I wasn't your typical street-hustler; all they knew was the block. I been in the game since I was fifteen years old and, much as I love gettin' this money, basketball would always overshadow most other things in my life.

- - -

– Pro-AM –

Two days before the opening Pro-Am games at Fox Middle School, and my team had the season opener with game one of a double-header. On my way to Keney Park to shoot around, I spotted Ozzy heading that same way. That turned out even better – at least now I had someone to beat up on while I'm out here.

"What's the deal, lil' brah? I see you got your Nikeys tied up."

"Yeah, you know what it is. Summer ball is here, and I'm ready to shine."

My team was being matched up with one of the best, if not the best team in the league. The kid, Tyson Wheeler that played for Rhode Island also Edmond Saunders, from UConn, was some of the talent on the other team.

I wasn't seeing any of them cats because they were gon' have their hands full with me. My man, Ozzy, had a task on his hands. He was teamed up with some ballers himself. Birdy, K-Y, and Dice were some of the best ballers coming out of Weaver High School.

For the next two days, I got ready for all of the media-hyped confrontation between some of the best that CT had to offer. The Pro-Am is one of the biggest summer basketball leagues, State to State, Pro, college, high-school, and neighborhood ballers; they all came back to their home State to showcase their skills. This year wasn't any different, and it was the best time of the year for me.

Putting on for my city is what I did, and when I stepped on to the court everybody knows what time it is. Showtime is what I am going to give you. This year was different though. This year, all I wanted was that championship. The competition was tough this year and I knew I had to step my game up if I indeed wanted to win the chip. Last week, me and my and my boy Keon was talking and I told him that we gotta get that chip by any means necessary.

- - -

– Thursday Night –

An hour before the game, and I am as ready as I am ever going to be. When I walked through the front doors, the gym was jam-packed. I hollered at the Great One for a minute and dapped up a few of my peoples. Inside the locker-room, the coach was going over the game plan.

I loved the big games, they turned me on. The starting lineups were announced, *"And at 5'9" tall, one of Hartford's finest point guards, King Thomas!"* Both teams circled up for the tip-off. My center, Eddie, tapped the ball to me, which left Tyson Wheeler the task of checking me.

For the first play of the game, I called my own number. I hit Tyson with a crossover, followed by a hesitation dribble that stood his ass straight up. Driving to the hoop, I took flight with a finger roll over the outstretched arms of Justin Brown, a seven-foot center from UConn. The crowd went crazy as we dropped back into our 2-3 zone.

They swung the ball a few times, and Tyson found Will Solomon in the corner for an uncontested three-pointer that he nailed. The game went back and forth for the entire first half, until they went on a 15-3 run to close out the half. I ended the half with fifteen points and six assists.

Getting off the bench for the start of the second half, all I could hear were Meth and God telling me to stay focused, to keep doing my thang. The other team possessed the ball for the second half. Tyson dribbled down-court and we were now in a full-on man to man press.

I was on him tight. Once he crossed half court, he tried to throw a lazy bounce pass to his left. Sticking out my right hand, I stole the ball on my way down the middle of the lane for a two-handed dunk. Before you knew it, we were on a 15-0 run of our own.

Calling a timeout, they tried to stop the momentum that we had. The squad stacked with some of the top college stars were being stunned, I seen it in their eyes. I overheard their coach telling Tyson and Will to stay in front of me; that let me know just how much they feared me.

The game was slipping away from them as we lit the gym up, raining down and sinking shots from everywhere. At the five-minute mark, I had thirty points, thirteen assists, and five steals. Chants of *"MVP! MVP!"* were being yelled out by the crowd.

We ended up winning the game 96-87 and I posted my first forty-point game of the year. After my game, I went to the locker room and took a quick shower. I put on a fresh pair of black army fatigue that I had packed in my bag; then I hurried out back to the gym and grabbed a front row seat to watch my lil' brother Ozzy play his game against Big Dog, Munk, Tuck and Animal. Ozzy did his thing leading his team to a 10 point win.

- - -

– Mano E Mano –

One week later, the day was finally here – the big game between the Thomas Brothers. Our entire family was in attendance for this one. Tonight, everyone would be getting more than they were ever expecting.

– Game Time –

Both teams came out ready to ball out. Me and Ozzy dap each other up and wish one another a good game. Most of the time when me when me and Ozzy stepped on the court together, it was as teammates. Both of us were looking forward to this match basically to test our skill set; it was playing against myself when I played my bro.

Both teams entered the middle of the court for the opening tip-off. Ozzy's team won the jump ball. My squad opened up man-to-man and Ozzy drew first blood. Ozzy dribbled the ball down court and a few step across half court; he pulled up and shot a three-pointer from deep with me dead in his face. "SWOOSH!" All you heard was the crowd yelling as Ozzy back step down the court in defense. I was awe-struck seeing him just disrespect me like that.

It was nothing big though because I came right back at him with an Allen Iverson crossover that made him jump back and lose his footing. Seeing that he was off balance, I gave him a hesitation move and beat him to the basket for a reverse lay-up. Running back down the court I told him, *"It's on now! Show me what you got, Lil' brother!"*

128

The game continued at a fast pace, with both of us hitting big shots and dropping dime after dime to teammates. This moment was something me and Ozzy looked for all of our lives. We'd played against each other numerous times, but this one game had so much meaning to it. He was, and he always will be my little brother, but his game on this court showed me that there wasn't much little about him anymore!

At the present time we were equals, and our basketball games showed that. We were both winners and we didn't want to lose this game even if we were playing against each other. Everyone could see that in the way that we both displayed our exceptional talents.

Going down to the wire, the game was tied, with Ozzy holding the ball for one last shot. 5 ... 4 ...3 ...2 ..., he rocked me side to side and pulled up an eighteen-footer that hit the bottom of the net as time expired. The entire family stormed the court, congratulating us both on a hard fought game.

I ended the game with thirty-one points, eleven assists. Ozzy finished up with thirty-eight points, nine assists, and the game winning shot in my face. The family wrapped up the night with a meal at Red Lobster, all expenses paid by me, for being the losing Thomas boy.

Chapter Twenty-One

-King & Skyla-

Last night, Ozzy and I really got it on the court. Even though it ended up being a losing effort for me, I felt good about the game. Kik ain't lil' Brah no more! He showed me that on the court. All the hard work and teaching I've given him is paying off.

Now there's someone else for me to teach, and that would be Skyla, my daughter. She's been watching me very close lately. I've been seeing her picking up a lot when she's practicing.

This morning when I looked out the back window, she was working on her game. We had the basketball court built out back a month after we moved in. Skyla was playing for the girls' basketball team at the YMCA.

"Skyla! You coming to eat breakfast?"

She looked towards me as if to say, *"Hell nah! I'm having basketball for breakfast."*

"No, daddy. I'm not hungry," she said.

"Girl, you ain't never hungry when you playin' ball. Come on, you need to eat. That ball ain't goin' nowhere."

I sealed the deal when I told her I'd play with her when we finished eating. Twenty minutes later, we were both staring at clean plates. For someone who wasn't gonna eat, my little girl sure was hungry.

"Daddy, I'm finished. Come on! Let's go play, you promised."

"Aight, baby girl, let's go."

"I'm gonna do you like Uncle did yesterday," she joked, rubbing it in.

"Oh, I see. You were ridin' with your uncle, huh?"

"Yeah, but I was goin' for you too."

We headed out the back door and Skyla ran right to the ball. *"Daddy, watch this!"* My girl did a dribble move that I swore had her looking just like me. She pulled up and shot a three-pointer that was nothing but net. *"See, daddy. Just like you and uncle Ozzy!"*

We started a game of one-on-one. Taking it easy on her, I let Skyla beat me ten to nine. I knew she was playing a lot because of the game she had tomorrow. I looked up and caught Sky in the window; she'd been watching us the entire time. I walked back into the house.

"I see my baby beat you out there," she teased.

"Girl, she got lucky. Plus, I was takin' it easy on her," I replied.

"Whatever. I just hope you remember her game tomorrow."

I was so proud for Skyla and was also relieved that I didn't have to pressure her to play. Like me, she just has a natural love for the game. I just had to bring it out of her. She was a Thomas,

131

and basketball was in our blood. My only hope was that she would not ever put too much pressure on herself, because sports will have you people nervous when you have to play in front of a crowd of.

- - -

– Skyla–

When I got up this morning, all I could think about was my basketball game. It's my first real game, and my dad and uncle have been helping me practice for it, and I really want to make them proud. Mommy and daddy were still in their room sleeping.

I wanted to wake daddy up so that he could practice with me, but I heard him come in late, so I knew he'd be tired. In the end, I just let him sleep. For some reason, he always comes home late these days, but he still comes by my room to check on me. Even when I wake up, I still pretend to be asleep, because I know he's trying to be quiet.

I ended up going out by myself and did a little stretching first to get my body loose. Daddy says it keeps you from getting hurt. I listened to him and my uncle carefully, because I wanted to be good in every way, that's why I listened to them carefully.

Daddy was hard on me, but that was only because he wanted to bring out the best in me. Even though I was only eight years old, I still had very high expectations for myself; I wanted to be the best. Grandma Queen said that I reminded her of daddy, because I was so strong-minded, because I was a leader, just like my daddy. I knew sooner or later, that daddy would hear me bouncing the basketball and come out back with me.

– 20 Minutes Later –

Sure enough, daddy was exiting the back door. *"Good morning, Skyla,"* was the first thing that he said.

"Hey, daddy! You up, hope I didn't wake you. I was just out here getting ready for my game tonight."

"Nah, you ain't wake me. I got up to use the bathroom, that is when I heard you out here playing."

I and daddy played around for a while. He had me doing dribbling, shooting, and defense drills. Not wanting to tire me out, we finished up after I shot some free-throws. We knew all the noise outside woke mommy. We smelled her cooking, and we were both starving, so we went inside.

"I was just coming out there to get you two," mommy said. Well, I sure was glad. I dug straight into my plate. French toast, bacon, eggs, and cheese. Daddy didn't like it when mommy fed me pork, but I loved to eat it! Besides, I don't wanna be skinny like those two.

"Skyla, ready for your big day?"

"Yes, mommy," I replied.

"Skyla, if you keep eating all that pork, you gonna be too big to play basketball," daddy said, teasing me.

"Boy, stop lyin' to my baby like that!" Mommy said, ready to pop daddy's head.

"Skyla, don't you listen to him, 'cause we eat meat, unlike him, and that's the problem."

– Game Time –

Arriving at the YMCA, I was more than a little bit nervous. I also had butterflies in my stomach. The gym was packed with kids and grown-ups. Mommy, daddy, and the rest of the family were all seated together in front, in the first three rows at half court.

Winning the opening tip, my cousin Tasha passed me the ball. I was the point guard, so my job was to run the team. I passed the ball to my center, Kelly, and she laid the ball off the backboard for the first points of the game. The other team was bigger than us, but they didn't have a good dribbler and that gave me the ability to steal the ball from them.

The game was very competitive and the crowd was really into it. Every parent was cheering on their child, but mommy was the worst; she was jumping around like crazy when I made a play. One time, daddy had to hold her back; she tried to run onto the court after I got fouled hard!

At half-time, the game was close. We were only up by four points and in the second half, the game got even tighter. Not noticing that the butterflies in my stomach were gone now, I was hitting shots from all-over like I was in my backyard with daddy.

The coach substituted me out of the game for some well-deserved rest. When I left the game, we had a fifteen-point lead. Now, with just four minutes left, we were doing our best to hang on to a five-point lead. *"Skyla, let's go! Get in there for Toya,"* coach yelled, patting me on my back.

One of the girls on the other team got a pass and hit a three pointer from the top of the key. Our lead was down to just two points. Dribbling down court, I beat everyone to the basket for the layup, hearing the whistle blow as I was being helped up off of the floor. *"Foul! Number twelve. Count the basket, Thomas shoots one free-throw,"* said the referee.

Getting up off of the floor, I looked to where my daddy was and smiled at him. I hit the shot and put us back up by five. With time just under a minute left, my team was holding the ball, eating the rest of the clock. When the horn went off and the clock showed all zeroes, the whole team was jumping with joy.

We had just won our very first game. My game was awesome, it was good to have my whole family come out and support me. I felt like the happiest child in the world, and I didn't want this day to ever come to an end.

Chapter Twenty-Two

It was mid-day, and the summer heat had the streets of Hartford scorched. It felt like it was over a hundred degrees today as Roxy and I sat in the passenger seat cruising around the 'hood' getting money and hustling. We drove through numerous blocks in the STS. The streets of Hartford were alive, full of people out and about; people who acknowledged us on every corner we turned.

As we approached the 24-Hour on the corner of the Avenue and Bedford Street, I eased up on the gas and pulled over. The 24 was crowded, so I decided to pull up and stunt on the block.

I gave Roxy some money to go inside and get me a fifth of Remy and a box of Dutch Masters. When Roxy got out of the car, all eyes were glued to her. Standing five feet, nine inches tall, her long, thick and beautiful legs were smooth as buttermilk.

She was wearing booty shorts that hugged her plump, curvaceous ass. Roxy's body was just right; she was Urban Magazine material. The matching top she wore was cut just low enough to show the right amount of cleavage; cleavage that would send niggas and a few females gasping for air.

The whole hood knew I was getting to the money. I was in the streets, and reaping the benefits of money, power, and respect. I was still fucking with Sky, but there was something about Roxy that I just couldn't get enough of. She was sexy, and her sex game was like that.

Whenever I would tell myself that I needed to fall back from her and be faithful to Sky, I would remind myself that I was still young and in my prime. I watched so many of my men catch bids out here in these streets only to see their broads run off on them with some other nigga. I was going to have fun, to live my life in the moment and think about the consequences later.

I stepped out of the whip and looked into the eyes of my cohorts and people I knew passing. I was acknowledged with either a dap or a head nod. The crowd of hustlers, bitches, and friends were checking me out closely. I was decked out in a pair of cream-colored Polo slacks and shirt and some size nine Butter Timberlands.

I was making my way over to holler at my nigga Petey when I heard a female voice calling my name. *"Hi, King."* The female said, looking my way. I kept my stride, but at the same time, I turned my head so that I could see the Pretty Young Thing that was calling out to me.

Sharonda was a sexy, young chick that had been on my radar for a minute now, but with everything going on in my life, I had her on the back-burner. Sharonda was sweating me like crazy. When she noticed I wasn't coming over to holla at her, she waved and continued on with her girlfriends.

"Yo! What's good, my nigga?" I asked Petey.

"Ain't shit, my nigga. Kik, you out here winning. You got Roxy fine ass with you. What? You inserted her into the starting line-up?"

"Nigga, you know me. I only keep bad bitches on the squad. She my new all-star chick."

I kicked it with my man for a few, and then made my way over to where Sharonda and her girls were. She was caught off-guard when she felt someone approaching her from behind. Turning around, she found herself face to face with me. She excused herself from her conversation, not wanting me to hear that my sexy ass was the topic of conversation.

She was just standing there, all dumb-founded, acting all nervous like she didn't know what to say to me. I broke the silence and asked her how she was doing. I let her know how good she was looking, and she really was looking good – but she knew my playboy ways, and probably thought I was just tryna feed her what she wanted to hear.

I was just hooking something up for her to call me later so that we could get together for some fun, when Roxy came strutting out from the store. Roxy glanced over to the car and didn't see me in the driver's seat. Searching the surrounding area, she spotted me talking to Sharonda, all up in her face, like we were a couple or something.

"This nigga know he got me fucked up," Roxy told herself, as she walked up on me and this female. *"Boy! Stop playin' with*

me, and let's go, before somebody gets trashed out here on this Avenue!" She shot Sharonda a devilish grin, letting her know that she was talking about her. Roxy turned and walked towards the car, not once turning to look to see if I was following.

I was laughing inside as I watched Roxy's ass jiggle from side to side. She wasn't wifey, but she demanded wifey respect, especially when she was out with me. Still on the bullshit, I looked back to Sharonda, signaling for her to hit my cell-phone later on tonight. She signaled back that she would, and watched as I got in the car and pulled off.

"I hope I fucked up yo little shot of pussy! Yo ass got too many bitches out here in these streets," Roxy stated.

"Woman, stop playin' games! You gotta come better than that if you gon' stop my pussy flow."

I pulled up Edgewood Street and parked in front of the vacant house across the street from the Blue House. I split open a Dutch while Roxy poured us both a cup of Remy. Roxy wasn't a smoker, so she just sipped her cognac and watched as I blazed the Purple Haze.

–Later on that Night–

King was chilling with Roxy at her crib on the East Side. Him and her son Polo were sitting around playing Madden on PlayStation 2. Polo was a couple of years older than Skyla. He had become as close as a son to King and he was a good kid.

139

Polo had taken a liking to King, that's why he loved whenever King came around. He thought King was cool as hell and felt comfortable talking to him about anything. *"What yah think yah gonna play games all night? Polo, it's about your bed time anyways,"* Roxy stated as she walked into the living room.

"Ahh, ma! We just getting started," Polo protested.

"Boy, don't play with me. Now, go upstairs and bathe so you can take your ass to sleep. You know you got school tomorrow."

"Dang, ma!"

"Boy, don't ma, me."

"Yo, stop talking to Kik like that," King chimed in.

"Boy, please."

"Polo, go ahead and listen to her mean ass. We gonna finish up after school tomorrow."

"Aight King. I guess I'll see you tomorrow then," Polo said and started up the stairs. *"I'ma see you tomorrow, kik,"* said Polo. *"Boy, get yo ass outta here, talking about kik. You ain't no kiko,"* Roxy said glaring at her son.

Hours later the kid was sound asleep and Roxy and King were lying in bed watching television. *"Roxy, you know you my heart, right?"* King asked as she lay cuddled up next to him.

"I hope so! I know you got all these hoes out here in these streets checking for you."

"Yeah! But I'm cutting' them broads off for you, ma."

140

"Well, we'll see," Roxy said with unbelief showing in her voice. King placed his hand inside Roxy's panties and played with her throbbing clit. She laid there and enjoyed his touch.

"Whose pussy is this?"

"Yours," Roxy purred.

"Whose?" King was flicking her clit back and forth.

"This yo pussy, King. God, you bout to make me cum," Roxy cried as she cum all over his finger. King positioned himself behind Roxy, while on her knees with her ass tooted up in the air. He pushed his meat deep inside of her pussy, amazed at how tight and wet she was.

"Oh, yes," she panted when he worked his engorged cock all the way inside her. *"It feels so good. Please fuck me harder!"* Their bodies smacked together making loud, sexy sounds as King pushed in and out. Roxy matched his strokes, throwing her ass back like a wild woman. King could feel his nuts tightening up, signaling he was ready to cum.

"Take this dick, ma!" he said, thrusting his dick deep into her pussy hole. She clawed at the blanket and moaned in satisfaction as his own orgasm subsided. The two lovers laid together afterwards, exhausted and fucked out of their minds.

Chapter Twenty-Three

God pulled away from the jewelry store in Downtown, Hartford. As he drove down Main Street he fingered the 40-inch, 24-carat chain that was flooded in flawless diamonds. As he passed through traffic, people tried peering through the dark tints to catch a glimpse of the figure behind the wheels.

It seemed as if every passing vehicle and walking pedestrian was staring his way. Females were pulling along the side of his whip, trying to get a look at who they assumed could only be a drug dealer. Honking their horns did no good, because God knew they were trying to holla, but he was just drinking in all of the attention.

He turned right up Garden Street and a white Suburban pulled up right onto his bumper. The truck had a light tint, so he could see four occupants inside of it. The driver and the passenger looked familiar, but he couldn't quite place their faces. He couldn't get a good look at the two individuals in the back seats.

God took a few random right and left turns, up and down different streets, and the truck followed closely behind him. He had no doubt he was being tailed, and was starting to think that they were stick-up kids, so he reached into the glove compartment and grabbed his 17-shot glock. He placed the gun on his lap and prepared himself for their move.

It was typical behavior in the city for robbers to tail their licks for a while before actually making their move; little did these robbers know that they were dealing with the devil himself. God is one of the best at this game, and he had no problem going out gun blazing if need be.

God made another left, down Enfield Street. *"If these ma'fuckas bend this left behind me, I'm gonna make my shit bark,"* he mumbled. Sure enough, the Suburban bent the left onto the field. This time, they pulled up on his driver's side. He aimed his pistol. The passenger's side window rolled down and the moment got intense. *"Dawg! Hold up! This yo' boy!"* yelled Crusher.

"Damn, nigga! I almost added you niggas to my body count," God stated, lowering his weapon. *"I thought ya'll were on the other team."* Damien looked over from the driver's seat, *"God, what's up with you, my boy?"*

God got out of his car and the occupants watched as all of the gold and diamonds he was wearing shined in the light. He was rockin' a black leather Avirex that sold for just under three thousand dollars.

"Damien, you already know what I'm on. I'm out here gettin' this money."

"Yeah, I see you. You looking good. Ridin' around in big whips. It must be nice."

"Man, this ain't shit."

"Yo! I heard about that shit that went down with the Germans from the South End."

"Yeah, that was some bullshit, them niggas tried to pull on my people. Yo! But what's up with you niggas? Fuck you doin' around the way?" Damien and Crusher were from new Britain, CT. Usually, when they were in the 'hood, they were tryna cop some work.

"God, you know I fuck with you, and we go way back. I got this little bitch I fuck with on the South End. Shorty was pillow talking, and she mentioned how them niggas was salty about Chucky's death. Rumor is, they gettin' together a team to get back at you and your guys."

"Good look, but this is the game we play. We already hip to them 'Ricans, they can come and get it," God stated.

"God, I hear you, Dawg! Just remember, I still owe you one for that lick you put us on the last time. Favor for a favor."

Before departing, God thanked the men again and then he pulled off and left skid marks in the middle of the street. Damien and Crusher looked on as God peeled out, knowing the time would soon come for them to repay the debt that they owed God and his team, but God ain't know that it would be as the opposition.

- - -

Back on Da Woodz, Meth was in front of the Blue House, talking to Darnisha. The block was doing its normal thing, money-wise, with fiends coming through at a high rate. He'd been out here on the block since earlier this morning.

Solid and Shiest were up the block, in front of Moosey's crib, while Milly and Forty were parked in Forty's Acura. Kat and Nelly were catching all the sales that came into the Blue House to get high. Prince was circling, catching sales off of his phone, and King had just pulled off with Roxy, heading to the east.

"Darnisha, when you gonna stop playin' and let a nigga get in those panties?" Asked Meth.

"As soon as you get rid of all of them other bitches, that's when," answered Darnisha.

"Oh, that's all it's gonna take?"

"It don't really make me no difference, but you won't be gettin' none of this good pussy until then."

Meth knew that she was dead serious too. They had been cool since high school. All the flirting they been doing over the years, and she ain't gave the goodies up yet. That quality alone was the main factor that made him want her so bad.

So many of these broads out here was quick to fuck for a get high. Darnisha was young, black, and beautiful; far from the average chick out here on jump-off status. Meth knew that if he really wanted her, he could have her, so that's why he kept her around and showed her mad love.

145

Meth recognized a green Lexus turning onto the block. He stopped talking to Darnisha to make sure his boys all peeped the unknown vehicle turning down the street. It was a must that everyone stayed on point with all of the bullshit that's been going down lately. He dismissed Darnisha, so that he could get back to business.

"Darnisha, let me get at you later, ma. Maybe we can get together and get really acquainted."

"Boy, bye! You still playin' these high school games. You gonna look up one day, and I'ma be taken by the next nigga," she stated before walking off.

When the Lexus pulled up in front of Meth, the driver's face came into view. It was his boy Dajuan, from off of Bluehills Avenue. *"Meth, what's poppin', big boy?"* Dajuan asked.

"Ain't nothin' my boy. Just out here gettin' my money up."

"Ya got this shit pumpin' out here. I need some of what ya got them goin' cuckoo for."

"Yeah! We pushin' that straight drop out here, and we got big rocks." Meth stated as a customer pulled up in a station wagon.

"That's what's up."

"Nigga, I been hearin' yo name ringin' bells real loud out here. You got Bluehills on the map, you know the streets talk too much."

"Man, don't believe everything that you hear. A nigga decent out here, but shit ain't moving like the shit is over here."

Meth and Dajuan politicked for about an hour, talking about different moves they both could bring to the table. Dajuan was amazed at how much money had come through since he first hit the block; fiends were pulling up in bunches and all of the hustlers were eating.

After a while, things were getting too hot, and a couple of police cars even cruised down Albany Avenue, watching all of the action that was going on. Dajuan had peeped both cars, and decided that it was a good time to get ghost, before the block got rushed and he got caught out here on the humbug.

Chapter Twenty-Four

-Birthday Blessings-

July 13 arrived, and it was closing in on midnight and I'd been out on the grind for the past two days without going home. I had plans of doin' it big for my birthday, but didn't really have any specifics planned.

Stumbling into the house after midnight, it was dark, and there was soft music playing. It was coming from the master bedroom. Peeking into my daughter's room, I was surprised to see that it was empty, so I figured that maybe, her and Sky were both in our room, still awake, waiting on me.

To my surprise, when I opened the door, I found myself staring at my girl, lying across a bed filled with rose petals, champagne on the table, wearing some sexy-ass lingerie.

"Happy birthday, daddy! I've been waitin' on you. How do you like your gift?" Sky asked. She was wrapped up in a bow, just like a birthday gift. Guessing that Skyla had to be over at one of our family member's houses, I was anxious to go ahead and start my birthday off with a bang.

As soon as I fixed myself to take my jacket off, Sky sprung off the bed and was on me like a bitch in heat! Ripping off my fatigue shirt, she was now kissing my chest while I lay on my back across our king-sized bed. I was now tugging at her clothes, but she was stopping me, telling me to relax.

"Daddy, I got you. Let mommy take care of you," she said maneuvering her tongue, sucking and biting on my chest. She had my dick ready to explode. I needed to be inside of her. Through the sheer lingerie, I could see her breast and her pretty pink pussy lips between her legs. I was just craving to bend over and beat the pussy up.

Sky unclasped her bra to expose those beautiful tities. I put my hands up and those melons dropped into my palms. I began caressing and sucking back and forth on them, sending her moaning into a state of bliss. Sensing that she was relishing in the orgasmic feeling that I was unleashing in her, I gently slid my hand into her thong, playing with the pussy.

The way my fingers played with her clit, one would have thought she was being fucked with the thickness of my manhood. The way she was riding my hand, you'd have thought it was her day until she grabbed the eight inches that was dangling between my legs and wrapped her mouth around it.

Holding my manhood with both hands, she went up and down on it with her tongue, softly blowing on it and causing sensations that were driving me crazy. Seeing that she was enjoying the moment, I laid back and allowed her to please me until I couldn't take anymore.

Pulling her up so that she could sit her dripping wet pussy on my manhood; she rode my shit like she was riding a bull at a rodeo. With my manhood deep inside of her, I was hitting the walls with every stroke.

Taking every stroke like a pro, she started quivering and biting her bottom lip as cum started shooting out of her pussy and down my leg. Bending her over so that I could hit her doggy-style, I held on to her ass and started banging her from the back. Cries of satisfaction; she was calling for me to give her more and more.

Two and a half hours into my birthday, my wife and I were having multiple orgasms, sending me to the edge as she inserted me into her mouth one more time to give me the last orgasm of the night, *"Happy Birthday, King! I love you."* were the last words I heard before drifting off into a deep sleep.

– July 14th –

When I awoke, officially a year older, and feeling the part, there was no sign of Sky anywhere. I jumped in the shower to freshen up and begin the journey for the day. While I was getting dressed, I heard the keys turning the lock to the front door and heard Skyla screaming my name, *"Daddy! Happy Birthday, daddy!"*

My little girl sounded so cheerful that she had me blushing. I came out of the bedroom and planted a big, wet kiss on her fat cheeks. After I finished getting dressed, we made plans to go out and eat breakfast, spending the first part of the day together. They knew that once I left their side, there was no telling when they would see me again.

After breakfast, we decided to go and spend some time at Kenney Park at Sky's request. It was noon, and for some reason, Kenney Park was crowded to capacity. *"Damn, Sky, I know it's summer, but what the fuck all these people doin' out here?"* I asked.

I started seeing friends of mine and Sky's; not knowing if it was coincidental, or if I was being set up. Setting my eyes on the basketball courts, I saw that they were also packed. Me being me, I took Skyla straight over there. They had music playing and everything.

I was disappointed, because I didn't have any b-ball shorts or sneakers. When we reached the courts, I was surprised by screams of *"Happy Birthday!"* and ribbons tied to trees which read, *"Happy Birthday King!"* Out of nowhere, my brother Ozzy came out of the crowd with a bag and gave me a big hug.

"Happy birthday, nigga! Open that shit and make it happen," Ozzy said. When I opened the bag, there was a basketball uniform that had "Team Thomas" on the front and my name across the back. Then my mom and my other five brothers stepped onto the court with their uniforms on. Sky, Skyla and Shelly had on jerseys too. I was teary-eyed with joy.

Meth, God, and Forty were at mid-court, making announcements about today being my birthday, saying it was a special day for all. They informed the huge crowd that food would be served and there'll be other activities, including this 40-minute game against "The Thomas Brothers" and some of the best talents the North End of Hartford had.

When I looked at the competition, I saw the Animal, K-Y, Bird, Block, and Dice. My young boys, L-Boogie and them were strapped up and holding it down. The game was like an All-Star game. We were all putting on a show, with me and K-Y going at each other especially hard. Things got real interesting when Queen put Skyla in the game.

"Oh, hell nah! My baby ain't goin' out there! She too small to be playin' with them," Sky hollered, looking in my direction. *"Mommy, I wanna play. I play with the boys every day at the YMCA,"* Skyla pleaded. She ended up winning the battle and was now on the court, displaying her talent.

Bird came down and got a pick from K-Y, and then found Dice cutting backdoor for a lob and flushed one down, two-handed. One play after another, both teams set the crowd to *"Ooohing"* and *"Aahing."*

Skyla stole the show when she came down dribbling the ball with Block checking her. I saw her lookin' for somebody to cut to the basket, but K-Y was draped all-over me. I happened to get lost by running him off a solid slip screen by Vince. Perfectly timed, Skyla hit me with a no-look bounce pass that I caught and threw down a one-handed thunder dunk that shook the whole rim.

Coming back down the court, Tuck tried to go for a layup, but Ozzy stripped him. He hit Prince with the outlet pass and Prince finger-rolled the ball in. The crowd was going crazy. With thirty seconds left, the crowd stormed the court.

I had Skyla up in the air while everyone walked up, giving her a dap. Both teams dapped each other and I was congratulated and showered with birthday wishes and compliments on the game.

I was proud of my family and my friends, but it was my daughter that had me geeked up the most. She ran over to me and said, *"Daddy, you thought I didn't see you, huh?"*

"Baby girl, I knew you saw me. I just didn't think you was gonna hit me with that beautiful dime," I replied.

"I got that from you," Skyla said with a wide, beautiful smile on her face. We dapped each other up and went over to where the food was to get our grub on. While I was eating with Skyla, people were everywhere mingling and kids were indulging in all type of games.

Skyla saw a group playing basketball on the miniature basketball hoops and asked if she could go play. *"Yeah, go ahead lil ma, but be careful,"* I said. *"Okay, daddy,"* she replied, and ran towards the court. I watched her from a distance for a minute, and yeah, she was killin' 'em. Feeling herself from the game we'd just played, she still had the jersey on so that you couldn't tell her shit.

I ran across Roxy chilling with a few of her girlfriends. I kicked it with her for a while, knowing Sky was around and that I

153

didn't want her on the bullshit, not today, so I made plans to see Roxy later on in the week. Before my departure, I gave her a brief hug to let her know that she's still recognized by me.

It was getting late, and people were starting to head out of the park. I was getting tired and sweating bullets, ready to leave myself. Once Sky, Skyla and I got home, the only thing that was on my mind was taking a hot shower.

Sky told Skyla to go and take a bath in her bathroom, because she was going to my mom's house for the night with her cousins. My mom loved to keep all of her granddaughters with her. I thought she loved keeping them because she never had a daughter of her own.

Shortly before I got in the shower, I received a phone call from my nigga, Meth. *"Yo, Kik!"* he said. *"What's poppin',"* I said. *"Hey, yo, Stage East is having a party, and the crew is goin'. Everyone is bringing their significant other. You should come,"* Meth recommended. *"I'll be there,"* I said before hanging up the phone.

I told Wifey what the plans were for the night, and we both took a shower and got fresh for the event. I had on my white and gold print gator shoes, white slacks, and a matching shirt. I was jeweled up and my mouth was shining bright. Sky was decked out in gold and white, matching her complexion.

We pulled up in front of Stage East in the gold Azure. Stepping out of the whip, both of us looked good, and all eyes were on us. My whole crew was up in the spot, showing out; bottles everywhere.

The women had us dancing all night. Sky knew I wasn't the dancing type, but since it was my birthday, I rolled with the punches. My birthday turned out to be one of the best I'd had in a long time, if not the best ever.

Through all of the bottles and blunts I went through, I was mellowed out. When it was time to go, I gave Sky the keys to the Bentley to drive us home. That was going to be the first and the last time I'd ever be a passenger in my own Azure!

Chapter Twenty-Five

-The Day After-

On July 15th, the day after my birthday, once I got my shit together, I headed out the door to start my day. I glanced out the window and saw that there was a car parked in my driveway. I was tripping, thinking to myself whose shit it was, because it was hard body. Going back upstairs, I asked Sky, *"Who parked their whip in our drive?"*

"I dunno," she responded. Vexed and not knowing what the fuck was going on, also hoping like hell it wasn't a stolen car, I went outside to see what was up. It was nice, I'll say that. A closer look at the whip, I found out it was a brand new, white 2003 Twin Turbo Chevy Corvette, sitting on 22-inch Forgiato Andata rims and Pirelli tires. There was a note under the windshield wiper which read:

"Whomp Star, Rude Bwoy, Happy Born Day! As you can see, this here is a present from the I. I and I is back in the States and remembering your born day and wanted to send you this gift. Hope you accept it. I and I is back up and running so when you done burning the tires, call my phone so we can burn some ganja. One Love, Tiger"

Damn, this nigga Tiger just bought a nigga a 2003 Vette. Man, niggas better watch out now. God better know I'ma be at his

Camaro RS! I was on my way to eat lunch when an unknown number rang my phone.

"Yo, who dis?"

"It's Roxy. How you doin', stranger?"

"What up, baby girl. I'm fine, how are you?"

"Fine. Could be better. If I was with you right now," she replied.

"Is that right? I was about to grab some lunch, you hungry?"

"A little. Where you gonna eat at?"

"I was thinking Outback," I said, knowing that was one of her favorite dining spots.

"That sounds good, King."

"So, you want me to pick you up?"

"Nah. I'm up and by myself. You hittin' the one in West Hartford?"

"Yeah, meet me there in an hour."

I was on my way to meet Roxy for lunch. I knew the Outback had good food, plus it was in the West, away from the 'hood. I pulled up and entered the restaurant. I looked towards the foyer and saw Roxy waiting patiently for me.

She had on some Dolce & Gabbana jeans that were showing off every curve. I was sporting a Roc-A-Wear outfit and a Yankees cap over my freshly corn-rowed hair. On top of that, I was blingin' from neck to wrist.

We were seated in a cozy booth inside the restaurant. While waiting on our order, we snacked on an appetizer. Roxy ordered steak and fries, and also a cocktail mixed with strawberries.

I ordered a glass of ice water, knowing I had a pint of Remy in my back pocket that I'd be pouring into my glass. Roxy thought I was crazy or something, *"Why didn't you order anything to drink?"* She asked, smiling.

"This is what I drink," I replied. We both laughed, and waited on our order. This being the fourth official date that we'd had, shit just naturally flowed. We talked about what was going on in each other's lives, homes and kids. Knowing that I was still with the wife, I could tell she wanted to be a bigger part of my life. The timing just wasn't right.

She was a good, independent woman, with two kids and her own shit. She was my type and I was diggin' her and her style. She looked at me and said, *"I want a man who wants me for more than just my looks. I want somebody I can share everything with, start a family, settle down."*

We were around the same age, but were far from being young boys and girls. *"I haven't been with anyone since we were together a few months ago,"* she continued. In my head, I'm saying, *"Damn! What, you savin' the pussy for me, or somethin'?"* Noticing that I was in deep thought, she interrupted, asking,

"What's on your mind?" Tipsy off the Remy, I regrouped and said, *"You're something special."*

Every nigga I know wants a bad-ass female that's going to hold her own and will ride with a nigga to the end. That was a rare thing to come across these days. Every nigga needs a backbone that won't break, because the female is already mentally and emotionally strong. To me, that was Roxy.

She was just what I was looking for in a woman. Don't get me wrong, Sky had mad qualities, but she stayed on a nigga. She'd stress a nigga over bullshit. Still, she was good to a nigga, and that's why a nigga got mad love for her.

So, when I look at Roxy, that's the only thing that keeps me from really fucking with her. We finished our lunches, tipped the waitress, and walked out to the parking lot to get our whips. I kicked it with her for a minute; then we made plans to hook up on the weekend.

Chapter Twenty-Six

Now that my connect was back in the States, it was time to turn up the heat on these streets. I'd talked to Meth and God a while back about this power move and now it was time to see if they were ready, mentally and money-wise.

Later on that same night, I got in touch with my two Kikos. I had them meet me at the house in West Hartford. While I awaited their arrival, I looked at what was laid out on the table: Dutches, a bowl of Haze, and bottles of Remy, Henny, and Bacardi 151.

As I puffed on a fat ass Dutch, the doorbell rang. I glanced out the peep-hole and spotted my homies on the other side. I let them in, dapping them up, and told them to make themselves comfortable. Them niggas peeped the bud and drink and immediately started to roll and pour.

"Damn, King! What? We still celebratin' your B-day?" God asked. *"Nah, I called you over 'cause it's time to get down to business,"* I replied. *"I told ya about my man. Well, he's back in town."*

"Who, Tiger?" Meth asked. *"Yeah, and he's ready to do something with me; something big. I need ya on this shit, there's some real money to be made,"* I concluded. I had Tiger ready to back me with taking over the streets by supplying major weight and muscle.

160

I told him I could handle the muscle part, but the weight was open for discussion. He was willing to drop as much work on me as I could handle. I told Meth and God I wasn't tryna get the work and sell it to them. *"So, what's the plan?"* God interrupted.

"I want to go in, get the work together, and build a foundation between us," I replied. Between da Woodz, Cabot Street, East Raymond Street, and all the niggas we fucked with, we could run these streets. We had that much ground to work with.

We were all young, thoroughbred niggas, that wasn't going for anything. My plan was to have the entire 'hood copping weight from us at a decent price, enough for us to eat without having to be in the light ourselves. If anyone got in our path, we'd crush them.

During the session, God said he was sitting on, like, forty stacks, Meth had about fifteen and some work that would put him at twenty-five, once he sold out. Last week, my brother Max told me that the money I had put into stocks wasn't doing so well.

The market took a nosedive, and my money got caught up in the process. I wasn't really trippin' about the money though, because on the low, the cash was for my brothers when shit got rough. My main concern was the money that I'd lost due to the lawyer fees and posting bond for me and my niggas.

I spent a lump-sum on the crib for Sky, my daughter and I. After calculating, I had to be sitting on a little over a hundred and fifty grand. I started adding up all the gwap I was spending on material shit. Knowing my connect was gone for a minute, I was still making money, but it wasn't really enough to get me over the hump.

- - -

Meth and God were ready. I could see the eagerness in their eyes. I told them I was going to set up a meeting between Tiger and the three of us. Letting them see that they were just as in this as I was, I let Tiger know that he could trust them as much as he trusted me.

The next day, Meth hit my phone and let me know he had twenty-five grand, and was ready. The meeting with Tiger was set for Thursday night, the day after tomorrow. Between the three of us, we had $215,000. Whatever we copped, I knew Tiger would front us the same, without hesitation.

I was well connected with him, so I really didn't need any money at all. He knew I could handle whatever, and I had proved that to him back when he'd left me that work when he went on vacation.

- - -

Thursday finally arrived, and all three of us were in my Acura and getting high before we went to holla at my connect. I got the call to meet Tiger at the Girl's Farm. When we got there, the club was just starting to get crowded.

We were ushered upstairs to an office that was heavily guarded by four rugged-looking dreads. They were strapped with 15-shot glocks sitting in fitted holsters. Once we were inside, we were escorted to an inner-office, where Tiger awaited with his right-hand man, who always accompanied him to any meeting he held.

He had boxes stacked on top of each other in one of the corners. From prior meetings, I knew we were leaving with bags of coke. I introduced my niggas to Tiger, and from the jump, you could sense nothing but love in the room. Keeping shit simple and getting straight to the point, Tiger let it be known that the work wasn't a problem.

He opened the boxes and showed us the raw, uncut coke stacked neatly inside each. *"Yah can take wit yah as much work you can handle,"* he confirmed. *"I got 200,000 in the stash spot in the trunk,"* I said. *"Ok, rude bwoy. Since it's three of you, I'm gon' grab three backpacks and load twenty bricks in each bag,"* Tiger said.

That left us with twenty bricks to get back at him with, to include a hundred-thousand-dollar debt. Twenty bricks at five thousand, that's a hundred thousand per twenty bricks, wholesale.

We all woke up the following morning, bright and early, and drove straight to the stash house to whip and pack up twenty of the bricks. Bringing back thirty bricks of fish scale, we all took ten bricks a piece. That meant we had to bring back 200,000 each.

It took about an hour for us to pack the other forty bricks and load them in the wall safe in the basement. Afterwards, we rolled out.

Throughout the rest of the weekend, money was flowing in from the three blocks we had the Kikos pushing on. Man, selling the bricks for twenty a piece, having the best coke at the cheapest prices, and supplying anything needed.

The money was coming in rapidly, and Tiger promised that he wouldn't sell other niggas work if we could pick up the business and bring in major paper. On Da Woodz, shit was flowing lovely. Kat was still holding the Blue House down. Vee went upstate to start his bid for possession of cocaine and a weapons charge. He'd been fighting his case, but the State ended up getting five years out of him.

I started kicking it with my brother, Prince, letting him know what was going on. He had lost his job, and was now off probation, so I started selling him big eighths at $2200. I told him to find someone loyal that could push the shit so he wouldn't have to be on the forefront. Between my brothers Nelly, Prince, and Kat, there was no controversy. It was enough money hittin' the block that everyone was eating well.

Chapter Twenty-Seven

-God-

I woke up to fresh air blowing through the open window of my condo, feeling like a Don. I had recently purchased the crib so that I could rest my head in peace and have somewhere to sneak off to. Now that the money was pouring in, it was time to relocate. No one could know where my spot was except for King and Meth. I had three bedrooms, two bathrooms, a three-car garage, and all the accessories to make it look exclusive. Let me put it like this – I was livin' in a baby mansion.

On my way to check the trap houses, I hit the Deuce and shit was looking good. I could see that the money was flowing, and my people were handling their business. When I pulled into the Shell, shit was off the chain. Bitches was pulling up in whips, checking out the ballers from the Ave.

While checkin' the honeys, I got a few phone calls from niggas wanting to cop some work. Knowing I didn't have any product on me, I made a quick run to the new stash house on the east and scooped up a few birds. King's man, Tiger, had the raw and the town was fiending for what we had. I was lettin' them go for twenty-five with no problem.

Jay, from Blue Hills hit me up for one, plus my man Jose from Park Street hit me for two as soon as I dropped the one off for Jay. Luckily, I'd grabbed three of them, and just took those two straight to Jose. If anything else came my way, I'd just hit Meth or King to see if they had something on the block, so I wouldn't have to make a trip back out to the east.

- - -

"Yo, Kik, what did I tell you about hustlin' out here if it ain't my work you pushin'?" I asked KB and Ted, two lames from over by Homestead. KB spoke up, scared to death, *"Man, we weren't sellin' shit. That cracker just pulled up on us and I ..."* Before he could get the rest of the lie out of his mouth, I hit him square in the jaw.

"Nigga! I saw you pass the work in the window! What the fuck you lyin' for?" I yelled. I was getting angrier by the second and just about to reach for my waist when Ted peeped it and spoke up. *"We apologize, God,"* Ted stated, scared shitless. *"KB! Bring your ass on, nigga"*

Ted knew how things could go once I got mad. My phone began ringing again. *"Yo, what's the deal?"* I asked into the phone. *"What's up, Kiko?"* Meth announced on the other end.

"Man, I'm here on the block. I just had to run that nigga KB and Ted off the strip, tryna catch sales."

"I dunno what's up with them two niggas. What's so hard about copping the work from us, then they can do them," Meth stated, feeling the same way that I did.

– A Few Hours Later –

Stepping out of the West Farms Mall after purchasing some gear that had caught my eye, I ran into Justice. Justice was an old partner of mine from Dutch point. Justice was big-time. He was getting major money out in Stanford. His main hustle was selling powder coke and he took flight once he hit the suburbs. We ducked inside Red Lobster across from the mall to catch up with each other.

"I heard shit's poppin' out there in the North End, yo," Justice said excitedly. *"I was on the verge to come and holla when the time was right."* Just the thought of running into God had light bulbs goin' off in Justice's head.

"What's the word, God?"

"I guess it is what it is. Shit on and poppin' on my end," I responded, letting him know it wasn't the time for gossiping. *"Oh yeah!"* Justice said, surprisingly. *"What's the ticket on that raw?"* He had a slight grin when he said this. *"Kik, 25,000 will get you the rawest coke on the East Coast,"* I said, returning the grin.

"Twenty-five, huh? What if I wanted a few of the joints? What would my ticket be?"

"Justice, I'ma keep it a hundred with you. On a scale of one to ten, this work is a ten-plus. You'll be gettin' it cheaper than me anything less than that. You like fam, so I ain't tryna make no change off of you. I just want to let you know that the work is official," I pronounced.

"Man, what kinda room do I have to get mine? I'm tryna spend 100,000. I'm goin' outta town tonight," Justice stated.*"Well homie, I strongly advise you not to miss out on this blessing. When I step out the kitchen, four bricks will become eight. And yeah, it's still gonna be A1,"* I said with confidence.

"Word!" Justice said, sliding his number to me. *"I'll have the gwap ready for four bricks in about two hours. Tops."* He stood there, with a zillion thoughts going through his mind, caught up in the numbers I'd just hit him with. At the same time, my mind was racing, because if I get him on my line, I'll look to profit sixty off of every hundred grand he spends. Plus, he's good, and I know he'll be hittin' me twice a month at least.

Knowing how valuable this nigga is, I can stamp him and say that he's *"Official."*.

– A Couple of Hours Later –

I sat in a rental car, parked at the carwash on Homestead Avenue, waiting on Justice; on the back passenger seat, sat a grocery bag that contained four bricks. Right on cue, and not even a minute late, a silver Navigator pulled up and parked alongside me. I peeped through the tint of his window; I could see Justice bobbing his head to his music. He stepped out of the truck holding a black duffel. I hit the door lock as he approached.

Once he entered the vehicle, he instantly spotted the forty-cal. sitting on my lap. I made the first move, grabbing the bag off the back seat with my right hand, clutching the .40 with my left.

"What's up, playboy?" I asked.

"Yo'. It's 100,000 in the bag there," Justice stated, passing the duffel to me. I opened and fumbled through the neatly stacked, rubber-banded piles of cash. Knowing that shit was good, I handed him the work so that he could inspect the goods.

After assuring that we were both satisfied with the transaction, we dapped each other up and then departed the carwash, going our own separate ways. After hitting a few corners and making sure I wasn't being followed, I headed to the stash house to drop off the stacks and grab some more work.

Chapter Twenty-Eight

-Highland Park-

I was going on a little vacation to Highland Park, just to get away for a while. Sitting in first-class on US Airways, I was hitting up different people. I had hit my nigga G-Money up a couple of weeks earlier about my coming to Michigan and doing something with him.

G. and I were like brothers; we went to middle school and ran the streets together. In our younger days, we competed over everything; girls, sports, hustling, whatever else there was. It was all fun and games though, and we competed to the best of our potentials.

– 11.30 a.m. –

As soon as the plane landed, I got off and retrieved my luggage from the baggage claim area. I spotted my nigga G-Money waiting for me by the exit. *"What's up homey? How shit been with you?"* I asked. *"I'm goody, King. What's up with you? Looks like life's doin' you good,"* G. replied.

"Yeah, you know me, G., ain't shit changed. Always chasin' that paper." We dapped each other up and left out the airport. G. was driving a 2000 black on black Yukon Denali. I

could tell he was doing his thing, because his swag was up to par, plus, he had that glow a nigga gets when that paper's bein' stacked.

– 1.00 p.m. –

We left G.'s brownstone on the east side of Detroit, heading to H.P. to check out my old stomping grounds. While driving, G. heard his cell-phone ring. As we all blew on some Haze that I'd brought with me, G. looked to see who was hitting him. It was another one of my long-time homies – Cash.

Cash was one of my niggas that would bust his gun, and we got good money together in the past. G hit the button on his phone on the third ring and passed me the phone.

"Fast Cash. What's good, nigga?"

"Yo, who dis? King?" He asked, surprised.

"You already know, dawg. How you?"

"I'm good, nigga."

"How the fam doin'?"

"My sister Kay doin' good. She's married and shit now. Jon doin' him, gettin' money on the low and fuckin' with that music shit. Other than that, everything else is good. How long you here for?" Cash asked. *"I really don't know. You know me, a couple days, a couple of weeks. I'm really on some business shit and tryna see what's up in the 'hood,"* I stated.

"King, I'm glad I caught you. You know I'm with whatever. Come through and holla at me," Cash concluded. I hung up

feeling good knowing that the old team was doing good. I had hit G. up a couple of weeks ago about me sliding into town for a few.

He put me up to speed about how the 'hood was off the chain since the Highland Park PD was put under investigation, about to get indicted. Shit, the precinct was closed down and the Wayne County Sheriffs were patrolling through Highland Park.

- - -

Within fifteen minutes, we were cruising down Hamilton Ave, high as a kite. Shit looked the same; my old side of the tracks ain't changed one bit. Turning down Eason Street, I spotted Money Ray, Mally, Deucy and the rest of the block niggas and females.

We jumped out for a minute and I kicked it with everybody. Word got around quick that I was back in town. I told Money-Ray that I was gonna holla at him about some major paper. He said he was down for whatever.

We headed over to Geneva Street, the block where I came up and made a lot of money. It felt good to be back there. Before we left G.'s spot, he slid me a chromed .45 automatic. Shit was still ugly out there, so I wasn't tryna get caught slippin'.

It was like a family reunion on the block, packed with bitches and 'hood niggas comin' out to see a nigga and showing some love. You know I was reppin' that Up Northeast Coast shit, but I was still in my element. I ran these streets and put work in for so many years, that my name and presence would always ring bells in this city.

– 10.30 a.m. –

Later that night, Cash, G., Chill, and I hit the cabaret at one of G.'s people's club and balled out. Entering the club, I noticed that the atmosphere and high-tech decor was dead on point. We were ushered immediately to the V.I.P. section, where bottles were iced down on the tables. Tables that were marked, "For The Big Homey".

There were bad bitches everywhere, some that I knew well, and some that I'd die to get to know better. We enjoyed the scenery, got high as fuck, turning up bottles, just having a ball. My vacation was starting off better than I even hoped that it would.

Out of nowhere, I spot this fine honey in the crowd, dancing all by herself. She pointed a finger at me, beckoning me to come over to her. I rose from my table and headed in her direction.

As I got closer, I looked into a set of beautiful eyes that I'll never forget. It was my old girlfriend from middle school, Laura. She was one of a kind. I'd had a crush on her since seventh grade. We embraced each other with a familiar hug.

"Damn, Laura! That's you?"

173

"Yeah, King. This me, your old girl! How are you and when did you get into town?" She asked.

"Oh, I'm good, maintaining. I just got in early this morning. I been fuckin' with G-Money and my niggas from old times, just catchin' up on the latest. I'll be in town for a week or so. Maybe we can get together and do lunch, or something?"

"That sounds good to me, here's my number. Call me. Anytime." Laura said sporting a sexy-ass smile. I wrapped shit up with her and headed back to the V.I.P. I glanced back over my shoulder and looked at Laura one last time. She was back with her friends, blushing, and feeling herself.

- - -

We left the cabaret and hit up the strip club. Broads were shaking ass everywhere! All eyes were on me as my iced-out diamond fronts sparkled off the disco lights. A waitress wearing nothing but a thong and pastie-covered, quarter-sized nipples escorted us to an open table.

A few minutes later, we were ambushed by a flock of topless dancers that must've seen nothing but dollar signs. Sensing that New Money had just set foot in the club, each girl was lined up and tryna get it. Before long, I was sticking bills in these two hoes' thongs – one black girl, the other an Asian bitch that was grindin' on my dick.

Chill and Cash followed five hoes to the fuck room, while me and G-Money were kept entertained by four other females. It was getting late and it was about time for us to shake the spot. I invited this sexy chick who only did sets onstage to spend the night with me. As soon as she finished her last set, I had one of the dancers go and get her from the dressing room.

About fifteen minutes later, the dark-skinned goddess strutted over to me and took a seat. We chopped it up for a while, then, next thing I knew, shorty was by my side and we were getting dropped off at the Marriot. I let G-Money know to pick me up first thing in the a.m.

- - -

Part two of my visit was about to be put in play. I was getting five of my H.P. niggas together to see if there was any money to be made, and if there was, were they willin' to get it? Tiger had a connect that worked at Greyhound, the bus company. He was a driver, who had routes going to and from Connecticut and Detroit and, tomorrow; he'd be stopping in the "D".

I purposely planned a run for this weekend. The plan was for him to bring work down in suitcases and the money was supposed to be ready for him to bring back twice a month. I needed to see where these niggas were at.

The work was A1 and it was enough for them all to push some major weight. The next day, I got up with G., Fash, Chill,

Steve and Jay. We politicked, and I let them know that I was in a position where there might be a lot of money to be made.

"Dog, niggas are ready to get this paper! Let's eat, King," Cash said. I felt the fire of the nigga I used to break bread with, day in and day out. *"B-EZY"*, my nigga, *"this shit can only go down if we all on the same page. I ain't tryna leave any of ya out. Everybody gonna get their own package. All I ask is that the paper be correct. This shit bigger than all of us,"* I said, looking each of my niggas dead in their eyes.

"Yo, what's the ticket on the work, King?" Chill asked. Steve was nodding his head, wanting to know the answer too. *"Chill. I'm talkin' major work, homey. The cheapest you'll find on the coast, and as much as you can handle. Now, depending on how much you can handle, we talkin' fifteen, maybe ten stacks, raw coke. Like I said, depends on what you can handle and how fast you can move the work,"* I said.

Shit was set up, and the homies was ready to get in. Before I dipped out of H.P. and headed back Northeast, I already had a shipment ready to touch down for my niggas. After kicking it with Tiger about expanding the network, I knew getting money in Michigan was a good look. It's money to be made and, while I was able to play the backdrop, I couldn't pass up on this one.

Chapter Twenty-Nine

-My Block-

All of the shooting that's been jumpin' off this week got the streets on high alert. You can see it in niggas' eyes, the money slowed up, and the cops were sittin' on the blocks, makin' shit hot.

I slept at the crib on Da Woodz last night because I'd gotten too wasted to drive home. Looking out my front window, I spotted a crowd of niggas at the top of the block, catching sales. Not recognising any of their faces, I strapped up with a loaded four-pound on each hip.

The crowd of youngins' that was standing in front of the bootlegger spot was cutting customers off before they could reach the Blue House. They were so caught up in the rush of fiends flooding them that they never even saw me run up on them.

"Yo, who y'all out here with?" I asked, pointing the two cannons at them. *"We out here on our own,"* a big, brave nigga replied. I almost shot his dumb ass, but instead, I hit him across his face with one of the four pounds. *"You young ma'fuckas better get the fuck off of my block before niggas start mournin' y'all ass!"*

The lil' niggas hopped into a burgundy rental, and marked off, taking the left down Homestead Avenue. When I headed towards the beginning of the block, shit was deserted. I thought niggas was probably in the Blue House getting money. Instead, I heard niggas talkin' shit in the back yard, shooting Cee-Lo (4,5,6.)

"Yo, King. What's up, bro? Man, I been hittin' 4-5-6 on these niggas all morning!" Prince said, looking at a pile of money that was sitting in front of him. As I stood and watched him roll, I watched him hit six head cracks quickly. He had Cutty, Milly, Solid, and D-Block all sick and quiet while he talked shit and took their money.

"Yo, y'all know I just had to run up on four niggas up the block for catchin' sales, right? Ya'll back here shootin' dice and ain't out here grindin'. What? I gotta get this money all by my damn self?" I asked, mainly looking at Prince, Kat, and Solid. Kat saw how serious I was and got up off her knees and headed to the front.

"We through gamblin' anyway. Let's go post up," Prince said to Solid. I rapped with Cutty, Milly and D-Block for a couple of minutes and then went up front with Kat. It was actually a nice day out, and the block was in full swing. Money was flowing up and down the block and, now that the gambling was over with, everyone was back on the grind.

"Solid, y'all missed a lot of bread while y'all was gamblin'," I said. *"Big homey, you right, but you know how Cutty and them niggas get when them dice come out. About them niggas hustlin' up the block, though. That shit's on us,"* Solid replied, realizing that was some foul shit.

Meanwhile, Solid walked off to serve some cracker in a station wagon. Feeling my phone vibrate, I answered and heard Skyla's voice on the other end of the line. *"Daddy! What you doing? Why didn't you come home last night?"*

"Hey, what's up, princess? I slept at the house on Edgewood Street. I was too tired to drive home. I'm on my way home now though, so ease up on your old man," I joked. My baby girl was getting older and maturing at a fast pace.

Ever since Sky bought her that cell-phone, she's been blowin' me up letting me know when I miss her basketball games and other family matters. She was right though; ever since Tiger came back, I've been runnin' the streets too much. She didn't know, I had a job to do, and there were a lot of bricks to be sold.

My team and I was tryna take over the drug game from the north to south ends of Hartford. Plus, Meth, God and I were gettin' sixty bricks every other Sunday.

- - -

When I got home, Skyla and Sky were in the living room, watching a movie. *"Hi daddy! You're home!"* Skyla exclaimed. She ran into my arms and gave me a big hug and kiss. Sky just sat there on the couch, looking crazy, like she ain't have shit to say to me.

"What's up, Sky?" I asked, still holding Skyla in my arms.

"Shit. Just watching television with our daughter," Sky responded

179

with more than a little attitude. Sensing that she had something on her mind, I left things alone, for now.

"Skyla, I'm about to go take a shower, baby. I'll be right out, ok?"

"Okay, daddy."

Five minutes later, Sky came into the bathroom talking shit, *"I met your lil' girlfriend at the club last night,"* she spat, almost sarcastically.

"What you talkin' about, Sky?"

"My cousin, Toya, is best friends with Miss Roxy's peoples and we ran into each other at the Pyramid."

"Girl, go on with that bullshit! Roxy is a cool person. We just friends. You ain't got shit to worry about," I told her.

"Yeah, I bet yo' ass probably be with her when you ain't been comin' home. Talkin' about you always at the house on Woodz," Sky intoned, sounding hurt.

"I told you about listening to your lonely ass friends. They don't know shit about me," I said, kissing her soft lips.

After a little slick talking on my part, Sky's argument dissolved into a full-on sex session. I had her trying to climb the bathroom walls. Still vexed and angry at me, all ill feelings escaped her mind as she took my manhood from behind, ass up in the air, moans turning into screams of passion. She was lovin' every single stroke I gave her.

After our sexcapade, I found myself in Skyla's room playing video games. My little Kik was no tomboy, but she loved playing sports and video games. She wore me out because we played every game she owned. I promised to play some ball with her if she'd take a nap first. Besides, her and Sky, I needed a little rest my damn self.

- - -

While trying to sleep, thoughts of Roxy and Sky kept running through my mind. Sky was the wife, and home with her was where my heart lived. Yeah, Roxy was a good person too, and I cared a lot for her. She was a wonderful person and I had some good times with her and there was a ton about her that had me thinking she was the girl I wanted to be with.

The relationship we had was good and respectful and made both of our lives better. Sky really needed to just chill, because if it came right down to it, she couldn't handle the truth. If she didn't know that she was the woman I loved, things were bound to get ugly, and her busybody friends could ruin our relationship.

See, being a big dog in the game, money, women, and all the material shit, it just came with the territory. Love and respect is what counts, no matter what. I'll always have those for her. Roxy and I were taking things slow, getting to really know each other.

A lot of bullshit with Sky was pushing me away, but Skyla always pulled us back together.

– Hood Niggas–

"Yo! Who that pullin' up in that Porsche truck?" God asked, pointing at the hard body truck. I took a good look and saw that it was my nigga, Heavy. *"That's that nigga, Heavy. He just came home a few weeks ago,"* I replied.

Heavy was another wild nigga who I'd come up from the dirt with. Kik stayed doing small bids, but for the most part, he got that paper. We grew up on the "Jungle" – Burton Street, when we were younger; me, him, and a few other heads. "Huntzone" was his stomping grounds.

I heard from a few niggas that my boy touched, and I know that getting money was the only thing on his mind. Shit, from the look of things, he wasn't wasting any time, either, seeing what he was pushin' around the 'hood.

"Heavy! What up, Kik?" I asked, givin' my nigga a pound and a solid embrace. *"King, I'm good. Back out here, doin' me, ya heard,"* Heavy replied. *"Yeah, what's up. Skyla been askin' about you like crazy, but Sky told her you were on vacation."*

Heavy and Sky were first cousins and Skyla loved when Heavy came around, because that was one more family member around to spoil her. We chopped it up for a minute, talking about mad shit; who was who, what was what, and what bitches was about their business. Shit was like old times, back when we were just little knuckle- heads, runnin' around the 'hood and doin' what knuckle heads do.

Kik ain't changed a bit. He was about to get his hair twisted by Maria. Typical Hartford nigga, cornrows to the back, mouth full of gold and diamonds from Steve. You knew who was gettin' money because everything was official about niggas.

"Yo, king. Let me get up in here and get my shit twisted. We gon' get up later, and do what we do," Heavy stated.*"That's right, Kik. We gon' do that. Keep yo head up, my nigga. That jail shit ain't nothin'. Our families need us out here,"* I said. I gave him dap, watched him walk into the shop, and I followed God back to Da Woodz.

- - -

– Meth –

"SAY YOU A GANGSTA BUT YOU NEVER POP NOTHIN', SAY YOU A WANKSTA AND YOU NEED TO STOP FRONTIN', GO TO THE DEALERSHIP BUT YOU NEVER COP NOTHIN' YOU BEEN HUSTLIN' A LONG TIME AND YOU AIN'T GOT NOTHIN ...DAMN HOMIE, IN HIGH SCHOOL YOU WAS THE MAN HOMEY, WHAT THE FUCK HAPPEN TO YOU, I GOT THIS SICKENED VENDETTA WHEN IT COMES TO MY CHEDDA', IF YOU PLAY WITH MY PAPER THEN YOU GONE MEET MY BERETTA, SHAWTY THINK I'M A SWEAT HER I'M SIPPIN' ON

*AMARETTA, I MIGHT HIT ONCE OR NEVER I KNOW I CAN
DO BETTER, SHE LOOK GOOD BUT I KNOW SHE'S AFTER
CHEDDA' SHE TRYING TO GET IN MY POCKET HOMEY AND
I AIN'T GONNA LET HER ... "*

I rapped along with 50-Cent's "Wanksta" from one of his
mix tapes. 50 my nigga, I know he gone fuck up this rap industry.
I was circling around in the Benz coupe, blowin' on Haze with the
windows rolled up, behind dark tints, checkin' out the 'hood.
Niggas was eating lovely all over, and you could see it in their
eyes.

Heading back around the way to check my own trap, I was
amped as a line of expensive cars came down the Ave. Benzes,
Lexuses and Escalades all came rolling slowly down the strip.
Them niggas had loud music coming out of the custom speakers
in each whip. They were all riding on 22-inch rims and had tints
so dark you couldn't see through them.

The only thing that gave them niggas up was the New
York plates. Niggas from the city was riding around the "Beat"
stuntin' crazy. They were ridin' high, and they wanted the whole
city to know it. Them niggas had to have something big going on.

I know they just ain't in the "Beat" ridin' and flossin' for
nothing. They probably had a show going on that I didn't know
about. Shit, there was no telling who the fuck was in those foreign
whips. One thing I knew for sure, though, whoever it was, was
gettin' major paper.

- - -

– God –

I slowly pulled up on the Avenue in my Acura coupe. My chocolate skin tone blended perfectly with black Sean John suit that I was wearing. Shiny bald head, with some diamond studded Cartiers graced my face.

Looking through limo tints, I was searching the house numbers on Colbrook Street, looking for China's crib. Towards the middle of the block, I found her house on the left-hand side of the street. I called her phone to let her know that I was out front. This wasn't my neck of the woods, so I needed her to be at the door and ready to let me in.

Minutes later, her front door swung open, and I made my way to the inside of her house. Walking into China's crib, I noticed that she was wearing a sheer nightgown with nothing on underneath. China didn't let me even get fully into the house before she was grabbing my pipe through my crotch area. She was in all-out freak mode, and ready to get her brains fucked out.

I delicately kissed her luscious lips, palmed her round, soft ass, and backed her onto the living room couch. My hand found its way to the front, and I inserted my middle finger into her pussy. Her wetness dripped down her thighs as I split her lips apart.

China fumbled with my zipper until she finally released my manhood from its threshold. Her clit began to thump from the friction as we ground against one another. I reached into my pants pocket for the condoms I'd bought at the Shell station.

She took the box and grabbed a condom, placed it on her tongue and proceeded to put it on my manhood with her mouth. After that little magic trick, I was rock hard. She dropped her pussy on my dick and rode me like she was in a rodeo. *"God, this dick is so good!"* She moaned. Her ass bounced up and down like a pendulum on my pole. She rode me like a mad woman.

China's pussy always seemed to satisfy a nigga and the slow neck kisses gave me a taste of what heaven must be like. After busting two nuts, it was time for me to get up out of here. Before I left though, I hit up Meth to see what he was getting into tonight.

"Yo, God! What's up? What's good with you?"

"Kik, I'm good. Yo' boy about to leave China's crib."

"I'm out here, great, chasin' this paper, like always."

"Meth, I'ma shoot to the crib and tighten up, then I'ma head around the way to fuck with you for a minute."

"Aight, I'm out here. I'll see you when I see you."

When I looked over at China, she was sleeping like a baby. Lying across the bed naked and sexy as hell, I pulled the sheets up over her to cover her up, checked my watch, and headed out the front door.

186

Chapter Thirty

Darnisha was at her house in Bloomfield, staring at the clock on her dining room wall. Meth was supposed to have been at her house over an hour ago to watch a movie, and she was starting to wonder if something had happened to him.

Now, she found herself pacing back and forth around the house. Her mind was racing in a million different directions, thinking about him. She stopped at the front window, hands on her hips, picturing his muscle-bound body. His smell, taste and feel drove her crazy.

The rush and sensation, mixed with the feeling of ecstasy had her pussy wet as a waterfall. It was driving her crazy, wanting him to be here, to be inside of her. Looking out into the dead of night, she felt herself losing hope.

Wanting to calm her nerves, she thought about taking a swim in the pool in her backyard. She tried calling his phone one more time, only to get his voice mail for the tenth time. She was at her back door and looking out into the cool breeze.

Darnisha undressed leaving a trail of her clothing until she was left in nothing but a bra and panties. The pool was huge, covering most of the backyard; rectangular in shape, with the feel of a community pool that was capable of holding about a hundred swimmers.

Kneeling down, she checked the temperature of the water before getting in. It was well after dark, and the water that had seemed so welcoming had that early evening feel. She put her left foot in first, and then the right, until she was waist deep. Seconds later, her whole body was underneath the water, as she swam to the deep end.

The pool always seemed to relax her when things weren't going right. When she got to the edge of the deep end, she rolled onto her back and floated along and looked at the sky. The shining stars shined like never before. She found herself trying to count each and every pin-prick of light sparkling above her, but every time she started counting, it just seemed like more were added to the endless multitude.

Darnisha pictured herself and Meth on the moon, having sex for hours. Thoughts of Meth made her horny again, and she slid two fingers into her love-tunnel and worked her pussy until she squirted her juices into the pool. After all of the time her and Meth been playing cat and mouse, she was finally ready to give him some ass. He had played her by standing her up.

- - -

– Stage East –

Stage East was lit up tonight. Everyone was out in Springfield, doing it up. Roxy, Rose, and Precious were amongst the sexy ladies that were out playing and partying. While everyone was on the dance floor, bumping and grinding, Roxy found herself at a table, getting drilled by her girls about her sex life.

"*Okay, yeah! Damn, if you must know, we been spendin' a lot of time together, but he's still with his girl. He said they are going through some things, though,*" Roxy said, feeling good about her role in King's life. "*Bitch, if you feelin' him like that, you better step your game up and claim his ass!*" Precious exclaimed.

"*What we gonna do? Talk about my love life all night or hit this dance floor and get our party on?*" Roxy asked, ready to shake her ass. They were starting to kill her buzz and she wasn't too thrilled about that. "*Girl, I dunno about Precious, but I'm with you, sis,*" Rose said. Next thing you know, they were on the dance floor bouncing and twerking to a fabulous track.

"*Stage East, we up in here!*" They all shouted over the sound of the music. Roxy was having some fun, and yes, while there were a grip of fine-ass niggas in the club, she couldn't front about it; King was on her mind and no matter how hard she tried, she couldn't stop thinking about him.

As soon as Roxy turned around to watch her sister, Rose, getting her groove on with some handsome dude; look who decides to walk into the club. Yep, you guessed right, King. And he was lookin' real good. Him and his boy Heavy were together and they were heading straight to the bar.

Seated at a table on the other side of the club, Sky was sipping on a cup of Patron, talking to her ex, Jayson. Jayson had been out of prison for a couple of months now, and was tryna push up on his old thing. They were tucked off catching up and getting to know what each one had going on in their lives.

Sky was so caught up in Jayson's charm that she didn't even know King was in the place and he had peeped her up to her no good shit as soon as he had walked in. Lust had washed over Sky as she dwelled in a state of comfort with Jayson. It almost felt like they were still an item until reality kicked her in the ass and she looked over towards the bar and saw Heavy and King with some girl all hugged up on him.

Almost erratic now, she told Jayson goodbye and got up and walked over to the bar to claim what was hers and hers alone. Roxy made her way over to the bar to surprise King. *"Hey stranger! Hope you're having a good time in here tonight. I sure am now that you're in here!"* She hugged him from behind and hissed in his ear. Spinning around on his barstool, King got up to return the hug.

"Roxy! What's up, doe? You love runnin' up on me in the club, huh?" King said, referring back to the first time they met at the Pyramid and she'd run down on him when he was with Forty. *"Boy, shut up!"* She replied, punching him in the chest playfully.

"Who you with, ma?"

"I'm here with Precious and my sister Rose, they're right over there."

"What ya drinkin'? It's on me."

"Whatever you drinkin', boo."

"Bartender, I'll have a fifth of Remy and two bottles of Patrol, for the ladies."

The bartender filled the order and gave them the bottles. King and Heavy walked Roxy back over to where the girls were, they joined them at their table and got comfortable. When Sky caught up to King, the group of five were now seated at the table, drinking and carrying on.

When Sky approached the table she got a rude awakening. *"Ma, don't even come over here playin' yo' self,"* King stated, cutting her off before she could even get a word out. *"Keep doin' you, and I'ma holla at you later."*

"Come on, Bae, that wasn't even what it looked like," Sky replied trying to explain herself; King wasn't hearing any of it. *"Kika, I said don't even go there with me, because I ain't tryna hear that right now. I'm on some new shit, so you can save that for that other nigga,"* he said continuing to kick it with Roxy.

Sky looked at Heavy and saw that he wasn't taking sides, she was super angry, and stormed off to go find her girl, Meka. Sky was ready to leave now. She knew she had fucked up, but she also knew that this would be the last time she let King cheat on her.

191

Chapter Thirty-One

This weekend was special for a lot of reasons. I was getting up with my boy, Big-O and some other ballers. Big-O was networking with some people in Detroit, but he needed a bigger connect. He'd recently gotten up with Cash; and Cash had put the two of us together.

I conversed with my connect to let him know everything I knew about Big-O. He was excited to hear how close Big-O and I were. The fact that I hadn't seen him in so long just made me more anxious to meet my long-time friend so we could put this shit together and kick the operation into full blast.

My flight will be taking off tomorrow at 11.00 a.m. I would arrive in the "Big D" on Thursday at around 1.00 p.m. It was late out, and I ain't been home since yesterday morning. I've been doing a lot of staying out, chasing that paper. I pulled up to Da Woodz to check the scenery before I took it in with the wife and my baby girl.

Shit was normal; Prince had the Blue House doing what it does. Solid and Kat was both outside doing their thing as usual. I went into Carlos's and paid for a box of Dutches and then headed home to my crib on the west.

- - -

Delaying the ride home by a few minutes, I stopped by the bootleg house to cop a fifth of Remy. As I pulled up to the spot, I sensed something suspicious in the cut. Before I could exit my whip, niggas were running up on me. Snatching the .45 from my lap, I made it spark, hitting the nigga on the driver's side in his chest and sending him to the ground.

BOOM! BOOM! BOOM!

Followed by the passenger window shattering, my attention was broughy to a second shooter. It was dark outside, and niggas was dressed in all black, so I was in a bad situation; I didn't know how many niggas were on me, or even who the hell they were.

My instinct had me roll-out the driver's door for cover, as shots continued to ring out. From a crouched position, I could see the second shooter, and with a clear shot, I took him out, leaving him leaking in the middle of the street. I didn't hear or see any more shooters.

I scrambled for a look at the shooters' faces as the sirens started to get louder. Heading back to the whip, I dipped out of there, thinking to myself, *"Was I being tailed?"* Paranoia was the enemy now. Escaping to make it home was my only desire.

- - -

After hanging up the phone with King a little while ago, I was feeling joyous as ever, because he was finally coming home. It'd been a few days since the incident at the club, and he hadn't come by to make sure things were good. Don't get me wrong, he calls all the time, and Skyla and I are used to it, but nothing beats daddy being here with us; where he belongs.

I was planning on cooking something small for Skyla and I to eat, but with King coming home, I planned on making him a full-course meal, and have him make love to me all fucking night long. I was just finishing up the meal when he stepped into the house.

One look into his eyes and I knew something wasn't right. Had his eyes not given that away, the blood and sweat on his clothes would have. *"Oh my God! What happened to you boo?"* I instantly knew something bad had happened because he had that far away stare in his eyes like he wanted to hurt someone.

"King! Calm down and talk to me, baby."

"Niggas tried to catch me slippin', Sky. I stopped at the boot-leg to get a fifth of Remy. Two niggas in masks came outta nowhere."

"Who were they after?" I asked cautiously. *"Just so happens I had my piece on my lap, because I knew shit could get ugly at any time. One of 'em snatched the driver's door open and I let off two shots to his chest before he could make another move,"* he continued.

"His man backed up and took cover, letting off some rounds. I was so in the zone that, before I knew it, I was on him,

hitting him in the head and chest. When I got back to my whip, I spotted blood on my arm, so I checked myself and saw that I had been grazed."

"*Did anyone else see what happened?*" I asked him. "*I don't know. I was just tryna make it out alive,*" he replied. Before our daughter came downstairs and witness her dad in the state he was in; I rushed him into the bathroom and ran him a hot shower.

Once I got him out of his clothes and under the water, I helped him shower. I tried to clean all the blood off him and find where he was bleeding from. Luckily, he was not hit. After the shower, King got dressed in our bedroom while I went downstairs to check in on the food. I called him and Skyla to the kitchen to eat, and pretended everything was just fine.

- - -

While the three of us ate quietly, still acting like nothing had happened, I thought about King. I knew he was a hustler by nature, but I needed him to be there for Skyla and me. Skyla was oblivious to the world he lived in, and she deserved more from her father.

I knew he loved us, but he was also in love with the fast money in those streets. What was it going to take to open his eyes and make him realize that only bad could come out of the life he was living? Skyla's voice brought me out of my trance.

"*Mommy, I'm finished eating, can I go play my video games?*"

"Yeah, go ahead, Skyla. And make sure your room is clean before you go to bed or I'll be waking you up."

King and I finished eating and then went upstairs. It took me about twenty minutes to wash the dishes and straighten up the kitchen. Before I got into bed with King, I went to check on Skyla. She was still playing her video games and had gotten her room squared away. It was spotless.

I tried to spark up my *"when are you going to leave the streets"* speech with King, but that got cut short with his *"as soon as I make my last move"* speech. I gave up on talking and started fondling him under the sheets. Seeing that I was turning him on, I eased under the sheets and started tasting his manhood.

He was erect and enjoying my touch. My plan was to take his mind off the streets and, by the looks of things, it was working. I was on top of him giving him head while my ass was facing him. He fingered my pussy, warming me up to get fucked. He kept telling me how wet my pussy was as he went in and out with his two fingers.

Feeling him start to jerk, I took my mouth off his still erect dick and sat on him cowgirl-style. I rode him until I cummed twice; he grunted, and I rose off of him. I got on all fours with my ass propped up, so that he could fuck my pussy doggy-style.

King gave me exactly what I asked for, he smacked my ass and took control of my pussy, plus he gave me orgasm after orgasm. He took all of his frustrations out on my pussy, and I loved every last bit of it. He was giving me the dick in a way that showed me he was concerned with the both of us getting our shit off.

He was also making sure that he made up for three days; the three days that he hadn't been here to fulfill his obligations at home. After we'd both cum in unison the last time, we collapsed into each other's arms, breathing intensely.

Holding on to King, I could only think about how wonderful he was. We talked for about an hour after our love-making session. I went to go check on Skyla and saw that she was sleeping like a newborn.

I went back to the room and King had the television on, tuned to Sports Center, watching the highlights. He said something about taking a trip to Detroit this weekend, but I only heard parts of his last statement, as I also drifted off to sleep.

Chapter Thirty-Two

Meth was packing his things into the back of God's truck alongside of my belongings. I decided to bring him with me to Michigan so that he could leave the east coast for once. Plus, it would be nice to have my right-hand man with me to assist and hold me down.

For some reason, the shooting last night wasn't even on my mind. I had killed them two niggas and never even knew who the hell they were. For all I knew, the only people left who even knew what happened were me and Sky.

One thing was for certain though; the two niggas were surely dead. I was holding the proof in my hands, on the front page of the Hartford Courant. It read: *"TWO DEAD IN WHAT LOOKS LIKE BOTCHED ROBBERY ATTEMPT."* I guess the police reached that conclusion based on the dark clothing the two guys were wearing.

- - -

At 11:00a.m., Meth and I boarded our plane. On the flight, I schooled him on the details. It was all good with him; he was just anxious to see how shit was in the Midwest. Later, when we got off the plane, Big-O was waiting for us in the busy terminal.

I introduced Uptown and Big-O to each other as we headed to O's ride. I was in my second home and had no idea just how long our stay would last. Big-O was getting money all over Michigan. He already told me about spots in Flint, River Rouge, and the east and west sides of Detroit. He also still had both hands deep in Highland Park's economy.

We drove out to Southfield, to one of Big-O's condos. Great and I were going to be staying here with him during our time in Michigan. The condo was plushed with flat-screens in every room. The living room was equipped with what was probably the biggest sound system I had ever seen. There were five bedrooms and two and a half bathrooms. The fireplace was ablaze and the living room was decorated to fit a Boss like himself.

Big-O showed us to our rooms and afterwards, we got our shit together and I hit the showers, to freshen up. After Meth and I got situated, Big-O called us downstairs to the dining room, where we sat at a round table. He had appetizers, assorted bottles of wine and liquor, and to top things off, there was a sandwich bag of Strawberry Kush.

- - -

"King, what's up with you? Long time since we seen each other," Big-O asked. I was good just being in the presence of the person that had taught me so much coming up as a youngster. *"Yeah, it's been a minute Big Boy,"* I said. *"I'm glad to have the opportunity to share a room with you again. I told my man Meth here how you*

brought me up from the trenches out here in these streets of Highland Park," I concluded.

"You know, you were my little solja, plus, you had the swag of an O.G. But it was your basketball game that I was banking on. I knew that with the right guidance you coulda been the first nigga from H.P. to get to the big league," Big-O stated with a serious look on his face. Hearing his last words took me back to my senior year at Highland Park High in '95-'96...

Geneva Street was where my mother, my four brothers and I lived. Being the oldest of the five, I was the father-figure at home. I was a baller in the dope game and on the basketball court. Whenever I had games, all the big boys would come to watch me play. *"Yo, King. When's your next game?"* I heard this question all the time.

Dawg never missed a game. He was there encouraging me, and I acknowledged that at all times. I remember leading my team out of the locker room with my uniform on and a basketball in my hands. When I looked out at the hundreds of spectators seated in the gym, I knew I had to do my thing. I always made sure that the crowd got their money's worth.

On top of that, I had one of the 'baddest' girls in the school, named Tonya. She was a "Dime", and I always had her by my side. A year younger than I, she had a high-yellow skin tone and stood 5'4" tall. To top it off, she was smart and loveable.

"Dawg, You alright?" Big -O asked.

"Yeah. Yeah, I'm good. Just reminiscing about the past," I replied.

- - -

We got down to some business while we got twisted. Big-O asked what kind of order I could fill, meaning how much work I could get him. I told him whatever the order might be; I could take care of it.

The days flew by and Meth and I stayed enjoying ourselves. I turned him on to some chicks that I knew from back in the day. He liked the way the people in Highland Park carried themselves. Ma'fuckas minded they own. Well, the majority of them.

I got up with my niggas from H.P. to check up on them. Shit was moving smoothly with them niggas. They were still getting their packages through G-Money. I was still sending work down here to him and he made sure the others received theirs.

When I made a call to G., he was at one of his spots on the west side of Detroit, off of Fenkall and Lasher. He had shit on smash all the way down Fenkall, between Telegraph and Evergreen. They loved that coke I was sending down.

Meth and G. got along good, too. Meth liked the way that G-Money moved. Meth just took everything in and didn't say or do too much, but he did recognize that he was around good niggas.

- - -

A week had passed, and we planned to catch the next flight back on Monday morning. Everything with Big-O was set up and ready. We made plans for him to cop 50 joints or better per month for a price, a price he couldn't have passed up even if he wanted to. It was a no-brainer, and Big-O was going to be locked in with some of the rawest work from the east coast.

Chapter Thirty-Three

A few days after returning from H.P., I found myself pulling up to a new, recently opened detail shop. The Escalade I was pushing was already immaculate, so I wasn't here for a wash and wax.

When I hopped out of the driver's seat, I was met out front by my nigga, Doe-Boy. Doe was a proud owner and newly legit businessman in the 'hood. "*Yo, what's goodie my nigga?*" he asked, giving me a pound.

"*Ain't shit, just out and about, circling the 'hood. You know how yo boy do,*" I replied, extending my fist out for the pound. I was proud of my boy, he'd come home and within a year, he had his own shop.

Kik was also fucking with Gates, promoting parties around the State. Being that the Hustle ran deep in his blood, he was still getting it on the side, pushing weight to niggas that was in his circle.

"*Kiko, I was just about to get at you. Business is lovely here at the shop, and I'm about ready to hit you up on that fish scale.*"

"*Do you, homey, and when you ready, you hit me up. You already know the deal,*" I said.

While we politicked, there were customers pulling up in all kinds of whips. Business looked real good from what I was seeing. We wrapped up some last minute details, and I departed the shop and headed to the spot to pick up some money from Prince.

Jumping in the truck, I fired up a blunt and listened to Fabolous' new mix-tape. I grabbed my phone and punched in God's digits and waited for him to pick up.

"God, it's me, Kik. Where you at?"

"I'm at the Hilton, laid up with this badass young bitch. Why? What's up?"

"Kik, ain't shit new with you. You stay in new pussy like I stay in new whips," I joked. Everyone who knew me knew how much I loved my vehicles, so you can just imagine how Kik played with them bitches.

I let him know that the pick-ups were all taken care of. I even went by his two spots and picked up the money his workers had for him. After a short conversation with my boy, I let him get back to his 'Pretty Young Thing' and I continued pushing the Escalade through the street of Hartford.

An hour later, I was budded out so high that I couldn't even drive anymore. Most of the heat that the law was putting on the 'hood had died down. Money was back flowing, and that was a plus, seeing how everybody's bills were getting paid. I was always big on my community, so giving back was a must.

Sponsoring basketball leagues and programs that the youth could participate in kept me relevant out here in the streets. Not everyone gave back, but my peoples were what I lived for.

Money changed nothing about me; it just gave me the ability to help my people, and that's exactly what I did.

After finishing what I had to do on the streets, I was mentally drained and in need of some rest. The touch of Sky's sexy and petite body would do me justice, so home was my next and final destination. As I drove to the west, Sky and Skyla were running through my mind. I was a lucky man, blessed with a good family to go home to.

When I entered the house, the aroma in the air informed me that Sky was in the kitchen and doing her thing. I went into the kitchen and found her looking good enough to eat. She was at the stove wearing nothing other than those booty shorts that I liked.

The popping of hot grease was music to my ears as she dropped chicken wings into the frying pan. She had baked macaroni and cheese sitting in the oven. She hadn't yet noticed me as I entered her domain and crept up behind her. Unnerved, but welcoming my touch, she let out a sigh of relief.

"What's up, baby? How my two girls doin'?" I asked, spinning her around so I could kiss her soft, inviting lips. *"We good, daddy. I'm in here cooking dinner, and Skyla's out back, playing basketball. She's been out there all day."*

Sky was about finished with the cooking, so she had me go and grab Skyla so we could all eat. Dinner was great; Sky put together a smash hit of a meal. I was stuffed from the wonderful meal Sky cooked.

Now, all I needed was some pussy, a hot shower and some well-deserved rest. Skyla obviously enjoyed the meal like I did because after she finished eating, she went to her room, took her bath and was now playing video game.

Sky eventually led me upstairs. She pulled me into our bedroom and led me by the hand to the king-size bed. She lay on top of me and started undressing herself. My hands roamed her body exploring each and every curve. Wanting it desperately now, she got up on all fours with her hands on the headboard, and bent over.

"King," she moaned, *"Give it to me…I can't wait no longer,"* she pleaded, crazy with desire. Fulfilling her wish, I spread her ass cheeks and eased myself into her wetness. I took it slow at first, stroking her passionately, as she pushed her ass back into me.

"Harder, baby! Fuck me harder!" she panted, wanting me to blow her back out. She seemed extra horny tonight, which only fed my desire and stoked my fires of passion. I rammed my dick into her and started fucking her like my mind was going bad. She returned my pumps for as long as she could, then she cum all over my dick. Afterwards, we laid up next to each other in a breathless and satisfying stupor.

- - -

Laid up in bed next to Sky, I was awash in mixed feelings. I can truly say that I loved her, but seeing her up in the next niggas face really hurt me. The kid wasn't a jealous nigga, not by a long shot, but the kid definitely wasn't no sucka. A nigga cheating ain't the same as a woman cheating, and that's just how it is.

I can deal with my lady not wanting to fuck with me because I was out here acting up. Me, King, I refuse to go out like that, so in the morning, when she wakes up, I'ma let her know that I ain't feeling that she even feels that she could let herself be up in the next nigga's face.

– Money Call –

Around two in the morning, my cell started blowing up.

"Yo," I said groggily, *"this King. Who dis?"*

"Kik, this Heavy. You out here?"

"Damn nigga, I'm laid up with yo' cousin on the west. Why? You need me? You know what? I'll be with you in a minute, if that's what it is," I said. I was in for the night, but for The Great, I'd come out. *"I'm on the Zone, and shit poppin' out here,"* Heavy replied.

"Gimme a half hour. I'm on my way."

"Aight, Kik. I'm out here waiting on you."

Being as I was ready to shake the crib anyway, my emotions were all over the place and chasing some paper was just the thing that I needed to do. Forty-five minutes later, I was taking my boy nine ounces of that flavor.

Heavy and a few of his men had Hunt Zone banging off the meat rack. I respected that my boy had come home and was still doing his thing. He was in one of the buildings, serving customers when I pulled up.

There was mad paper coming through the block tonight. I noticed a few of my regular customers out here trying to cop. The 'hood was like that, every block had many of the same crack fiends. Whoever had the best quantity and quality was gonna get all the money.

Chapter Thirty-Four

King pulled the Azure up Vine Street bumping "I Want To Be Your Man" by Zapp & Roger. He stopped in the middle of the block where he'd spotted Roxy and a few of her home girls chilling out.

"Bitch, who pullin' up in this expensive-ass car, playing my song?" Asked one of the girls in the crowd.

"My man!" Exclaimed Roxy with confidence. She was standing next to Precious and wearing a cheesy-ass smile plastered to her face. She watched as King gets out of the driver's seat and begins to walk towards her and her friends.

He leaves the car running and the music playing. He walks up with the aura of a boss. The other girls try their best not to stare hard at him, but the nigga was, indeed, all of that. He was wearing Gucci slacks and shirt, with some Gucci shoes on his feet.

The fifty-inch chain with the iced out clown medallion swung lazily from side to side, like a pendulum, shining in the light of the sun. He was fresh to death, and he knew it. Roxy stepped onto the sidewalk at the same time King did.

"Roxy, what's up, ma?" King asked, extending his arms for a hug.

"Ain't nothin', King. What's up with you?" Roxy fell into his embrace and kissed him full on the lips.

"I was tryna see what was up with my girl. I know tomorrow's your birthday, so I was thinking that tonight you might want to hit the club and spend the rest of the night with me and you doing whatever."

"The girls had plans for us to hit Stage East, but I can ride with you if you want me to."

"Yeah, that's what I want. I want everybody to know you're off limits, you feel me? So, I'll pick you up from the east at about 10:30 p.m."

"I'll be waiting ...With my birthday suit on," replied Roxy with a devilish grin. King pulled Roxy to him in one last embrace before he made his exit.

Entering his car, he got comfortable and prepared to pull off, but before he did, he fumbled with his CD player until he got to number six on his playlist. He peeled off as "Nothing in This World" by KeKe Wyatt, featuring Avant came on. *"See you later, ma,"* he shouts over the smooth playing music.

– Later That Night –

King and Roxy stood outside the club looking like the perfect couple as they waited for Meth and his girl, who said they were five minutes away. On cue, a black sedan pulled up and parked right next to the Azure.

Meth climbed out with his girl snuggled up close to him. Meth and King greeted one another with daps and a quick embrace. Their women also hugged up and said their hellos. *"Kik, what's good with you?"* King greeted.

"I see you lookin' good, wifey lookin' good."

"Great, you know how we do. Look at you and the birthday girl, looking like straight royalty."

"Hey Meth," Roxy said, giving him a hug.

The foursome entered the club ready to have a nice time. It wasn't long before the group was sitting cozy in a secluded area, popping bottles and having the time of their lives. Roxy's sisters and the rest of her crew were in attendance as well.

There were eight large tables, filled with bud and bottles of assorted brown and white liquor. After a while, the liquor was kicking in and stirring up all kinds of emotions as the dance floor was filled with partygoers getting their dance on.

"Dance with me, Boo," Roxy said to King as she got out of her seat and took him by the hand. *"Anything for my lady,"* he said, letting her guide him to the mass of souls moving on the dance floor.

From the moment they set foot on the floor, Roxy and King were the center of attention. Roxy was feeling extra good, as she ground her butt into King's midsection. She did most of the dancing, while King managed to two-step his way through a few songs. All around them, friends and family were turning up, tearing the dance floor to pieces.

King looked deeply into Roxy's beautiful eyes as she danced to "Could It Be" by Jaheim. He was thinking about his life up to this point and he thought he was living a good one; maybe not the best, but definitely blessed. He had money, he had cars, he had women and, most of all; he had respect in these grimy-ass streets.

He was gambling with his money by getting serious with Roxy knowing he had Sky in his life, but when he thought about it he was just young and living life. He'd happily give them the chance not to fuck with him if that's what they wanted, but he wanted what he wanted, and right now, that was to live like a boss, and get mad paper.

After the club, King and Roxy continued their special night by getting a suite downtown at the Hilton. Roxy happily unwrapped her birthday gift; lying back on the bed, she spread her legs wide open. King was on top of her, pushing her gift in and out in a slow, but teasing rhythm.

"King, I want you all the way up in me."

"That's really what you want, ma?"

"Yes daddy. Fuck me hard!"

Roxy brought her hips upward to match King stroke-for-stroke as he went deeper in her cunt, hitting her G-spot. King loved the warm wetness of her pussy and he felt as if he could fuck her for days; every stroke feeling just as good as the first. Their bodies intertwined perfectly, it was as if they were one in body and soul.

Roxy wanted to be frozen in time, in this moment, so that she could savor and relive it every minute of her entire life. She's never had dick this good, and swore an oath to keep this dick as her very own.

"Whose pussy is this?" He asked, slamming his pole deep into her core. For the rest of the night and early on into the next morning, the two pleased each other, only stopping to rest long enough to build up the energy they needed to go again.

Chapter Thirty-Five

The following day I was out and about trying to get to the bag. I was driving under the cool air condition and burning on some fruits "Purple Hazes." With it being almost a hundred degrees outside, I was surprised that people were outside in this heat. *"This must be what hell feels like,"* I thought to myself.

By the time I had made it to the north, the streets were jam-packed. The kids were out and running wild, cherishing the last month of summer before school started back. I headed over to the Hut to go holla at my man, Mancho, a Puerto Rican nigga from the projects who I fucked with.

As I pulled in, I immediately spotted him, shooting the breeze with a couple of his homies. I had first met Mancho in the mid 90's; during one of those summers I'd left Highland Park to visit Hartford. My pops lived in the Hut off Wadsworth Street with my brother Vince, my sister Shelly, and their mom, Helen.

Parking the Acura, I hopped out yelling Mancho's name. He looked over and recognized me instantly. We gave each other pounds as he welcomed me back to his neck of the woods. *"What's up, my nigga? It's been a minute now,"* Mancho said. *"What brings you around these parts?"*

"Kik, I was just out and around, and you came to mind. So, I stopped through," I said, noticing that he was happy to see a

nigga. While we were kicking it about what was going on these days, two redbones walked up, tryna holla at a nigga.

"What the hell ya want?" Mancho barked, upset that they had rudely interrupted our convo."

"Damn, Mancho! We were just tryna see who this fine ass nigga is you with," the thick one named Tisha said.

"Tisha, this my nigga King. And no, he ain't tryna holla at yo' fat ass," Mancho said.

Tisha gave him a look that could kill. *"Nigga, please! You just busy cock blockin' because we ain't checkin' for yo' weak ass!"* Seeing that they weren't going to get anywhere, both girls walked off, back in the same direction they'd come from.

"Mancho, I been hearing some good things about you. You been makin' plenty of noise out here," I said, continuing our convo. *"You know me, King. It's gravy out here, my nigga."*

"I feel you. Right now, I'm doing me and shit is poppin' with that work," I said. We mingled for a while longer. I asked respectfully about the prices he was paying, hoping I could line him up with some of my work.

He said that he was fucking with some Dominican from up top. *"I'm good, homey. I got somethin' already set up in the works. Unlimited work is just a call away,"* Mancho said, wearing a serious look on his face.

Sensing that he was starting to feel uneasy, I let him know that I just wanted to make sure that he was all good, knowing we were both getting it. I let him know some tickets, just to show some face. *"Do yo' thing, Kik, but just remember, shit's always on the table for you if you change your mind,"* I said.

Mancho went back over to the dice game and I headed towards my whip. By this time, the two redbones had approached me again. The one named Tisha was screaming about how she had been seeing me in the clubs around Hartford and Springfield.

I had to listen to her tell me how she'd been wanting to holla, but couldn't ever get at me for some reasons. She was kind of cool. She looked good, had a sexy face and a tight body, so, I ended up getting the digits and going about my business.

- - -

"Damn, bitch, you got some good tight pussy," King stated as he had Lulu's legs spread eagle on the bed. *"My pussy belongs to you now, King! Oohhh! Baby, it's yours! Fuck me harder, King,"* Lulu screamed out as her pussy gripped tighter as another powerful orgasm rushed through her body.

Deep down inside, King was feeling a bit guilty about fucking one of Sky's closest friends and in their house, on their bed, was a stretch, but Lulu threw the pussy on him, literally. Those thoughts and feelings quickly disappeared as he turned Lulu around onto her stomach, face down, ass up.

"I been waiting to get up in these guts," King said while giving her ass cheeks a firm smack, leaving red hand prints on her

216

fat ass. *"Well handle yo business great because I fantasized daily about you pumping that big ole dick inside me. Sky always talking this and that, how you be fucking her brains out. Give me that dick, nigga!"* Lulu begged.

King placed both hands onto her hips. Lulu reached back, grabbed his balls and messaged them as he fucked her dripping wet pussy. King pushed in all the way to the hilt. He pulled out slowly, and then rammed his dick back in fast and hard.

Lulu was loving every bit of hardcore fucking King was giving her. He pumped his eight and half inch dick in and out, like a mad man. He was dogging the pussy and Lulu cherished every minute of it.

She was used to fucking these lil' dick niggas in the hood, but what King was giving her was definitely gonna have her ass coming back for more. After another hour of fucking and three orgasms later, she was officially dick whipped.

Chapter Thirty-Six

-God-

I was at the Shell Gas Station posted up and doing what I do – chasing that money and entertaining a few bitches that was hanging out pocket watching, trying to find a baller to leech off. My guys Forty, Cutty, Milly and L-Boogie and a few of the Kikos were also out getting to the bag.

Though the day was rapidly going into night, the beams the sun was sending down made it obviously clear that it was still a hot summer day. The two MVPs that entered the Shell gas station from the Sterling Street entrance caught the kid's eye.

Through my Cartier glasses, I immediately peeped trouble on the rise. Spinning away from the homies, I gestured to the homies that something was about to go down. As soon as the two vans came to a halt, all the doors swung open, and eight masked men jumped out, equipped with assault weapons, and opened fire on everything that moved.

Things suddenly seemed to start moving in slow motion. Niggas were finding cover, getting out of the way of bullets that were intent on striking any target. I was the first to let off shots; at least enough to let these niggas know shit wasn't sweet.

The sight of two masked men hitting the ground, and shots coming from the back yards let me know that it was on and

218

poppin'. Not knowing that they drove right into a barricade, the masked men found themselves caught between a rock and a hard place. Their vehicles were the only cover that they had and there was no way out.

It was raining bullets and people were dropping like flies. The last two men standing tried to make it to the vans for a quick getaway but were cut short. Looking at the casualties, everyone looked to see if the danger was dealt with. *"Yo, son!"* Cutty screamed, running towards where I lay, my two .45s still smoking in my hand. *"Man, God hit!"*

Niggas moved on my location while Forty, Lil Mac and L-Boogie were already loading me in the back of the truck. Niggas didn't have time to wait on an ambulance; they just wanted to get me to the hospital.

I was a soldier, I fought through it, even though we'd just been ambushed and I'd taken rounds from an assault rifle to the torso, my right leg, and my shoulder. The kid been in mad shoot-outs in the early part of his life. One time I was shot in the leg while I was driving one of my whips.

This time was more serious. I could see my life flash before my eyes. I could see my team getting money without me, my family living without me, and the fact that I didn't have any kids let me know I hadn't even really lived my life yet.

Cutty blew every light and stop sign until he made it to Hartford Hospital. My condition was hurting everyone in the truck. Niggas was feeling that they didn't cover me, and that's why I was suffering right now.

Seconds after arriving at the hospital, I was rushed into surgery. I was tough and I pulled through. I had the instincts of a Vietnam vet in the way that I spotted danger. I actually saved a lot of lives while at the same time, almost losing my own.

– The Next Morning–

– King –

I was back at the hospital to see my boy. When I had gotten there yesterday, he was in surgery and we were all informed that we wouldn't be able to see him until this morning. I was really fucked up being that I wasn't around to aid him.

God was living and that's all that mattered to me. Him not being there with us, that wasn't even an option. When I walked into his room, he was laid back and watching Sports Center, eating breakfast. I embraced him lightly, knowing that he was bandaged up.

"God, what's the deal with you, soldier? The streets are sayin' the hood looked like somethin' straight out of an action movie, Tears of The Sun, or some shit," I joked.

"I don't know about all that, but the shit definitely went down yesterday. Niggas whipped up looking suspicious, so when I peeped the set, shit got poppin' from there," God said.

"I heard niggas unmasked them cats, but nobody recognized who they were or where they from. Had to be a big hit, them niggas was lookin' to do some serious damage."

"Kik, the detectives were up in here soon as I got out of surgery, askin' me all types of crazy shit. Who the dead guys were, who they had beef with, drug territory, all that shit, I Just told them pigs I ain't know nothin', and to keep it movin'. They said they knew that I knew more than I was tellin. Mother-fuckers acted like they wanted to charge me for the shit. What? They think a nigga's a Navy SEAL or somethin'? Like I'm gonna take all them mothafuckas out by myself?" God asked.

A few hours passed, and more and more visitors were showing up to check on God and show their love and support. Time was flying by and I had to go and meet Tiger for a pick up. After that, Sky wanted to see me and holla about a few things.

Chapter Thirty-Seven

-Months Later-

The club was filling quickly, as Hartford's finest walked through the doors, prepared to celebrate another day of life. Everybody that was somebody was out to show face, letting it be known that they were getting it.

Sitting in the parking lot behind the cover of tinted windows, Heavy and I were tucked in the cut and blowing on bags of fruits. We watched some of the elite enter; niggas from all-over the beat was out stuntin'.

The parking lot was loaded with the finest whips and the ladies were at least ten times the ratio, and they were looking the part. *"Damn, Kik! It's jumping out here today,"* I exclaimed as I grabbed the .40 cal and tucked it into my waist band.

"Good. That means them hoes gonna be actin' up. You know the kid gon' line something up," Heavy replied as he loaded his .45 with a full clip. We both exited the vehicle and walked up to the crowd at the club's entrance, heading right to the front of the line.

"Hold up, homey," mouthed the diesel-built bouncer as he held his hand out to stop us from entering. Not wanting to draw too much unwanted attention because we were strapped, Heavy pulled dude to the side. Kik peeled off two crisp hundred dollar

bills from his knot and the bouncer cleared the way and escorted us inside.

"King, let's hit the bar, get some bottles, and do us," said Heavy once we were inside. *"Yo, that's what's up. I got the bud and the Dutches. All we gotta do is find a table or a spot, so we can get it on and poppin',"* I replied.

In the midst of us stepping off, Kik fucked around and bumped some broad, causing her to spill her drink. *"Damn, boy! You ain't see me standing here or something? Yo' ass made me spill my shit,"* she said. Shorty ain't even give Kik time to say *"excuse me."* She just started snapping from the jump.

"Yo, that's my bad, shorty. That was an accident," Kik said, trying to ignore the disrespect that came out of ol' girl's mouth. Shorty, however, was on some other shit and must've thought she was talking to some offy-ass nigga.

"Yo bad? Nigga, look at my fucking dress! You ruined my shit!"

"Shorty, I said my bad and it was an accident. Now, miss me with all that other shit. What you want me to do? You want me to buy you another drink? I'll do that, but you keep talkin' that slick shit and tryna make a scene, you gonna make me get out my character."

Kik bein' the nigga that he was, Heavy was trying his hardest not to disrespect shorty, but she sure was asking for it. *"Ay yo, bartender. Get shorty a bottle of whatever she drinkin' on,"*

223

Heavy said, placing some cash on the counter. *"You good, Heavy?"* I asked, trying to make sure he was cool. Dumb ass chicken about to get herself jammed up, and niggas wasn't playing games tonight.

We sat back and watched all the people enter the club from a low key spot ducked off in the corner. We drank and smoked ourselves into a comatose state; all along trying to keep our focus on our surroundings.

It was a little after midnight and the spot was now in full swing. By now, me and Heavy were getting entertained by two sexy bitches. The darker and thicker of the two female eased up on Heavy and started dancing on Kik. Her girl then followed suit and started grinding her fat ass on me.

Looking over at my boy, I could see that Heavy was enjoying the girl's company; Kik was high as hell. I was in a zone myself; high on the drink and Purple Haze. Shorty was doing her thing on me. I had to ease my hammer into the small of my back so Shorty didn't cause it to fall or worse, go off in the club!

"Daammmmmm! You doin' it like that, ma? I see you just ran up and chose a nigga," Heavy said, watching shorty wiggle her booty to Nas' "Street Dreams". She said *"Well, I seen you over here, and there' no reason why a man of your caliber shouldn't have somebody sexy holding on to him."*

Four spins later, the ladies were sweaty and excused themselves, probably for the restroom or something. Niggas were out splurging, we ran into a few homies from around the way, acknowledged them, and kept on doing us.

Walking toward us, coming through the mass of the crowd, was a group of niggas. Leading the group of niggas was the loud-mouthed bitch that Kik had accidentally bumped into. Something in my head was telling me that shit was about to get hectic.

"Dion, there he goes, right there. That's the punk-ass nigga that bumped me and ruined my damn dress. "This chick was really tryna show her ass up in here; and these niggas were in a state of not knowing who they were dealing with. They were staring into the eyes of a cold-blooded goon in Heavy.

"Yo, my man. What's the deal with you and my girl? She says you bumped her and spilled a drink on her dress." Heavy and I could tell that these ma'fuckas weren't from Hartford because of how they talked, and the fact that they didn't have a clue as to who they were fucking with.

"Yo, my man, I told your girl sorry and offered to pay for the little outfit she got on, but she just kept running off at the mouth. Now, she got you runnin' over here like shit's sweet or something," Heavy stated through clenched teeth. Unbeknownst to the group, they had walked into a lose-lose situation.

The girl's boyfriend cocked his arm, ready to throw a punch and that was a mistake. Kik whipped out his .45 and, in mid-stride, connected to the right side of homey's dome.

225

"You dumbass nigga!" Heavy roared.

WHACK! WHACK!

"Do you even know where you at? Better yet, who you fuckin' with?" Heavy yelled.

WHACK!

Kik continued to assault the dude for the disrespect from him and his girl. I held Heavy down and brought my hammer into view, letting the rest of the crowd know how they could get it too. Partygoers looked on in shock as the loud music continued to rock the club.

The out-of-towner lay sprawled out on the dance floor as if he was dead, but a good ass-whooping had just done his dumb ass in. Pandemonium began to set in as the nigga's girl went into a fit of screaming. She fell to the ground next to her bloody and beaten boyfriend, trying to help him come back to the land of the conscious.

Semi-sober Heavy and I snuck out of the club and hopped into the whip before the cops showed up, and we ended up going to jail. Kik did a number on that kid in the club, but dude asked for it. He was lucky that the ass-kicking was all he got.

Chapter Thirty-Eight

King was strolling down the aisles of Stop & Shop, searching for some items that his mother Queen gave him to get for her. He heard a very familiar voice call out on him. King located the direction that he heard the woman's voice come from. Turning around, he walked over towards Monica.

King and Monica had something going on back in the days. It had been a minute since he'd last seen her. She secretly still had a crush on King since she met him again one day after clubbing at the Barbados Club.

Monica was one of them girls that could actually dance on a nigga's dick. She had some good pussy too. Monica would put on some R&B music and slowly grind her pussy on a nigga. She kept King coming back for more until they made it a permanent thing.

Now, seeing her today, King was thinking of the possibility of smashing. It was no secret that King wanted her badly right now, and he could see that she wanted the same. Before King departed, he made sure to exchange phone number with her.

King gave Monica a call later that night and she invited him over to her house. King was excited to hook up with her. He was thinking about all the freaky things they were going to get into.

Monica had got out of the shower and was slipping into a pink thong and bra set. She was rubbing Victoria's Secret body lotion on her chocolate skin when she heard the doorbell ringing. King had arrived just when Monica was finishing up.

Monica grabbed her matching pink robe and hurried to answer the door for King. She was greeted with a dozen red roses, a bottle of her favorite champagne, and a handsome smile. She eagerly invited King into her home. Monica gave King a hug and a wet French kiss. *"Thank you, daddy."*

In the process of greeting King, her robe fell off from her body, exposing nothing but her pink thong. Her swollen nipples brushed against his upper chest. She thought of how King was always an excellent kisser, his tongue caressed the inside of her mouth, making her pussy wetter and wetter.

She could imagine his tongue licking her clit and sucking her wet, slippery slit. But a thought was all that was; King was never much of a pussy eater. The tongue lashing was making her ready to cum right then and there! She pulled away, feeling the need to breathe.

Monica felt his dick getting rock-hard and pressing against her core. It took everything she had to keep it from tearing at his clothing. She collected herself and welcomed him into her home, told him to get comfortable, and then she went and poured them both a drink.

Sitting on her bed, they sipped champagne and, pretty soon, were lying comfortably next to each other, talking about the old times they shared. Small talk turned into sex talk and she positioned herself on her hands and knees, with her plump, firm ass sticking straight up in the air, and told King that this was how she wanted him to fuck her. She came out of her panties and he followed suit.

She was panting when she found herself being pulled back onto King and felt the head of his thick, stiff cock easing into her dripping hole. He drove his pole in and out, ramming it deep inside of her and then very slowly pulling out. It felt so erotic and sensational, she could hardly take it.

She felt her pussy grip down on his dick as it seemed to expand even bigger inside of her coochie. She reached down and behind, and grabbed his balls when she felt him starting to cum. Her pussy sucked his cock in as they both climaxed together.

They spent the whole night making love in every way imaginable. King was so worn out from Monica's sex that he was too exhausted to drive home. He decided to stay the night; and in the morning, they went some more.

- - -

Two months out of the hospital and God was back in action. He got up this morning, got dressed, and headed for the Buckland Hills Mall. As he pulled into the parking lot, he noticed how packed it was. It was Saturday, so there was no school and folks seemed to be out enjoying their weekend off of work.

His sound system was bumping Cam'ron and The Diplomats as he cruised slow, passing by people in the area. God parked the Escalade and made his way to the mall's front entrance.

"Damn! It's going down up in this bitch," God stated to himself. All he could see were bad chicks everywhere. He had a good eye and an excellent taste when it came to females, and they were in abundance today.

God walked towards the escalator and headed upstairs to Forever-21, where all of the females liked to hang out; right next to the food court. As he got to the top, he got off and looked around, seeing nothing but bitches everywhere. Most of them looked like young college students, so he knew he would be bagging something official.

"Man, I am glad I picked this morning to hit the mall," God said under his breath. He made his way through the food court and caught the eye of a bad-ass snow bunny with a few of her girlfriends. The girls were sitting down and eating as God walked by.

The snow bunny smiled, and waved his way. He stood there, Cartier frames on his face, smiled and waved back at her. Her friends caught on to her flirting antics, giggled, and started whispering something about him to one another.

God saw that at least the snow bunny was digging him, so he decided to make his move on her. He approached her, introduced himself, and asked her name.

"Hey, how you doing? My name's God, what's yours, if you don't mind me asking?"

"Jessica. And no, I don't mind."

"Jessica, huh? You lookin' really sexy in that outfit."

"Thanks. You're looking pretty handsome yourself."

"Well Jessica, I'ma keep it real, I'm tryna get to know you better."

"Well, we could start by exchanging numbers."

"I can dig that."

The two exchanged phone numbers and God promised to hit her up a bit later. After meeting Jessica and getting her digits, God did a little shopping and scoped out a few more honies in the mall.

Through all the shopping around for clothes and hoe-hopping, he couldn't wait to get back around the way and call Jessica. He had plans for her sexy, petite ass, and at nine that night, he broke down and gave her a call.

"Hello, may I speak to Jessica please?"

"Yes. It's me."

"Hey! This God."

"God who?"

"The God you met at the mall earlier. Let me find out some other dude's tryna steal my identity."

"Oh, the handsome black guy in the food court? The one with the ton of diamonds in his Cartier frames?"

"Yeah, that's God," he laughed.

"So God, what you got planned for tonight? All my girls are gonna be hittin' up a club. Maybe you can swing by my dorm and pick me up? I promise you, I'm a lot of fun to hang out with."

Within the hour, God had picked Jessica up from her dorm room and headed back to his Honey-Comb Hideout. Once they were in his room, God walked her out to the balcony and wrapped his arms around her tightly from behind.

Helping her out of her coat, he was shocked to see her wearing some white, see-through negligee that exposed all of her goodies. God led her back into the bedroom, where he began to strip her out of the negligee. Finding no resistance, he slid his hand to her pussy and found a tight slit just leaking juices.

Seeing God fully dressed, Jessica began to help him out of his clothing. She started with his shirt and worked her way downward until he was just as nude as she was. She got down on her knees and took his dick in her mouth.

God knew that white girls were a good fuck and knew how to suck some dick. Jessica did not disappoint; she was awesome at eating the dick. Before he knew it, his dick was jerking in her mouth, unloading his nut down her throat while she greedily swallowed it.

"God, I want you to put that anaconda inside me." He spread her legs wide and teased her by just putting the tip inside her. She was bucking off the mattress, trying to get more of his cock inside her. He then plunged farther into her silky-smooth, shaven pussy.

God filled her up with every stroke, and she cried out in passion as he pumped faster and harder, until he began to feel his load building up. Not wanting to cum yet, being as he wanted to punish this sexy snow bunny, he turned her around to fuck her from the back.

She gasped with delight at the new position. He dug in deeply, and pounded her hard. Jessica backed her ass up, meeting his every stroke. She was proving to be a good fuck. After a while, God felt his load building up for a second time. He slid his hands down to hold the front of her thighs, pulling her closer to him, pushing his dick into her as deep as he could.

He grunted and exploded deep inside of her. Her pussy muscles gripped and squeezed every drop of nut from him. Empty and spent, God pulled out and offered his dick to Jessica for one last blowjob and she again satisfied him, cleaning his pole with her luscious lips.

On the way to drop her back at her dorm room, Jessica continuously asked God when they would be seeing each other again. She let him know that he was the best she'd ever had. God let her know that he also had a good time and that he hoped to hook up with her again soon.

Chapter Thirty-Nine

"Homies, there that nigga go right there," Trigga turned his head just in time to get a glimpse of the black Impala that Crazy D had pointed to. *"Yo! Get the fuck in, bro! That nigga ain't gettin' away from us today!"* Trigga and his team of young goons were two cars deep following behind their mark.

They had been on the old head for the last two weeks, just waiting on the right opportunity to make a move on him. Big John had just gotten back into town from New York City when the young boys spotted him turning down Bobour Street.

He was clueless to the tail that they now had on him, and any wrong move he made would probably be his last. Turning onto Garden Street, he was nearing his destination. He was on his way to the gambling spot to shoot some craps.

Big John was a heavy gambler. Any given night, he was known to drop 10-25 racks at the dice game, so when Trigga seen the Impala's brake lights beam red, he knew they had to get at him before he made it up to the spot.

"Man! Fuck, yo!" Trigga screamed while banging the steering wheel in disgust. Before they could make their move, Big John was parked and out of his whip, toting a black, Fendi backpack, which most definitely was carrying a nice chunk of change in it.

He was beyond vexed. So much that he found a parking space, and vowed to stick up everybody that looked like they hit a lick in the spot when they left out of there. *"What? We gonna wait out here for that old nigga?"* Crazy D asked, starting in on Trigga with the rhetorical questions. *"Nigga, what the fuck it look like we're sittin' here for?"*

Meanwhile, inside the spot, Big John was the man of the hour. To call him lucky was an understatement. He was fucking the crap game around. Literally, he had been on the dice for an hour and a half.

The gamblers saw him walk in with the Fendi bag and every nigga in the place's eyes lit up. Now, almost two hours later, he was still on the dice, hitting number after number. The moment was all his and he was loving every minute of it.

"Man, this nigga got a rabbit foot up his ass," an old timer named Quincy yelled out as he backed off the fade. John had hit him in the head for ten racks in less than twenty minutes. *"Don't run now, big time. Stand under this gun like I stood under yours the other night!"*

Just the other night, Quincy had Big John's dick in the dirt as he wiped John out for twenty large. Now that the tables were turned, Quincy was taking his losses and tucking his tail. It didn't take a rocket scientist to see that Big John was on a mission to break the game, and now all he needed was a fader.

"Come on, now! I know there's somebody in here man enough to fade me," Big John declared, stroking his ego. *"Well, I guess ya gonna just let me leave with all this."* He loaded the Fendi with all the cash he had piled in front of him. From the looks of it, he hit for fifty thousand or more, bringing him to well over seventy racks in his possession.

Seeing that he wasn't gonna get a good gamble from anyone in the house, Big John packed his shit up and walked to the exit. He was sure that nobody in the spot would try anything, as they were mostly all his partners.

The gambling house was known to be off-limits for the fuckery, and that's one of the main reasons all the big boy hustlers and money getters frequented this spot. Big John made it outside, and to his car when he felt cold steel being pressed to the back of his dome.

"Old head, drop the bag, and don't make no sudden moves if you wanna make it home to the wife and kids tonight." Big John looked up slowly to see three masked men step into his view, not counting the one that had the hammer to his head.

"Young blood, just take the money. It's all in the bag. It doesn't hold no value to me. Just don't shoot me." As Trigga grabbed the Fendi bag from the pavement, Crazy D hit John on the top of his skull.

WHACK!

Big John fell to the ground and went night-night. Trigga and Crazy D jumped back into the half a crack, and his two partners did too. Trigga drove down Garden Street and made a left turn onto Albany Avenue.

Both cars drove through the night without a care that they'd just hit a lick in the heart of the city. They were living the life of stick-up boys. It was evident that jack boys made their money fats and often.

Their main marks were the hustlers that they knew wouldn't call the cops for fear of breaking the code and being labeled as rats. Thirty minutes later, they ended up at one of their homey's cribs in the Sands Projects.

After counting out the eighty-one-thousand-dollar score, Trigga gave his three homies ten thousand a piece. *"Yo, good look, my nigga."* They all thanked him. *"My niggas, there's much more if you roll with me. We gonna get this money off these suckas, or die trying."*

- - -

– Next Day –

King and God leaned up against King's STS, chopping it up about shit that was going on in the 'hood.

"Great, you heard about what happened at the house last night?"

"Nah, God. What went down over there this time?"

238

King figured something wild probably went down; the gambling spot on Garden was always a topic of conversation.

"Man, Big John went up in there dolo, and hit the game for like a hundred large."

"Word?"

"Great, that ain't even the crazy part. That nigga got robbed for everything once he got outside. He said some young niggas ran down on him as he got to his car and they were masked up and they just put them hammers to his head."

"Damn, Kik. That nigga just can't catch a break. I was in there with him a couple weeks ago and niggas beat him outta thirty racks. Old head needs to give that hustle up. Even when he wins he loses." King stated.

"Shit, whoever got his ass, they came up on some real shit. That was a good sting right there," God countered.

Meth turned onto Edgewood while "Oochi-Wally" by Nas and the Bravehearts blared through his speakers. He spots his two homies, God and King leaning up against King's STS. He pulled up and parked alongside of them.

The block is packed with people swarming around like there's a party going on. Crack fiends rush the block from all directions. From the top of the block to the bottom, each corner of the street is full of customers.

To a foreigner, things might look crazy, but on "Da Woodz," it's nothing but a normal morning. Meth looks across the

239

street from the Blue House where he sees Shiest in the drive, catching sales. All around him are fiends, patiently waiting to cop and go, so they could get high.

"Hey Shiest, baby. Let auntie get a wake up."

"Auntie, take this and get yo' ass off the block."

"Thank you, honey. I'ma run you some customers."

Meth gave Shiest a head nod then greets his two homies with fist bumps. The three of them kick it in front of the Blue House and watch all the action going on around them. Edgewood Street was always known to be a drug block, but the boys had this shit out here jumping.

The Woods was definitely a million-dollar spot. But with all of the wealth and fame, in came the envy and the hate, which brought beef and gunplay, and that was generally followed by senseless killing and, ultimately, niggas getting locked up because suckas can't take the pressure.

Chapter Forty

-King-

I woke up this morning and almost went crazy. My ass done let some pussy trap me and now I gotta hope Sky's crazy self ain't gonna be trippin' on a nigga. With all the shit we been going through in our relationship, I got no room to be getting myself caught up.

Things have been okay with us. I've been going home and staying the night on the west, with her and Skyla. That's really all she ever wanted, for a nigga to tome home every night. With all these missed calls from her last night, I already know it's going to take a lot of explaining to get out of this one.

Actually, I am sure it's going to take more than just talk to fix this one. I'ma have to stop at the crib on the Woodz and shower and change clothes. Going home to the wifey and still smelling like the next chick would be suicide.

As soon as I pulled up on Edgewood Street, my phone started ringing, and yes, it was Sky.

"Yo, what up, Sky?"

"Boy, stop playin' with me. Fuck you man, what's up?"

"Didn't you just call my phone?"

"Motherfucker, I been callin' your phone! All damn night, as a matter of fact. I know you seen all them missed calls."

"Yeah, I seen I had like twenty missed calls. I just woke up an hour ago and was on my way home, but it's so much money coming through this bitch."

"King, we could've had an emergency last night and you were nowhere to be found. Boy, this shit is starting to be too much. I ain't sign up to be a single mother with no baby father. We supposed to be a family. You act like you love them streets more than you love your own family."

"Sky, don't even talk like that. You know I love my family. I'ma wrap this shit up out here, and I'll be home in a couple hours."

"Alright, but make sure you bring yo' ass home. King, last night I had a dream that something bad happened to you, but when I woke up I couldn't put the dream back together. Like, I know it was something bad, because when I woke up I was screaming your name."

"Sky, don't worry. I'm good and I'll be home soon. Tell Skyla I love her."

– They Coming For Us –

Sky tried to warn me about some kind of danger she dreamed of, but couldn't recall any of the details. What is it they call that? A Woman's intuition! She was on to something, because in a matter of minutes, shit got serious out here on the block.

"Get the fuck on the ground and put your hands behind your head! Don't you motherfuckin' move, or I'm gonna blow yo' fuckin' head off!" It seemed like the United States Army had just swarmed the entire block. All I could see was armed officers with blue and yellow windbreakers with the letters "FED" spelled out on their backs.

The motherfuckers hit the block like they were invading Iraq. Once the Federal officers rounded us all up, they escorted us into the Blue House and things got even more real. *"Gentlemen, you have now graduated to the big leagues. Each of you, along with some more of your buddies, are being indicted on Federal drug trafficking charges,"* said the agent in charge.

I cannot believe this shit! The Feds? Everybody knows that when these motherfuckers get called in, there's gonna be some serious time getting handed out. It also meant that there were probably people lined up, and ready to snitch on a nigga.

Meth, Solid, God, Perry and I were put in one paddy wagon, while Cutty, Block, and the others were ushered into another one. Once we got to the federal courthouse, we were all taken to a courtroom where each of us had lawyers waiting.

When the Judge finally came in, the Prosecutors read off all of the counts that we were being charged with. My heart almost stopped once they got to stating that me, Meth and God were being charged with conspiracy to commit murder.

The drug charges were bad, but we could handle them, but murder? In the feds, that was guaranteed to land us behind the walls for life. After some counseling from our lawyers, we all pled not guilty.

The lawyers petitioned the court for bail and when it was all said and done, everybody got bail except me, God, Meth and Perry. They argued that we were flight risks due to the severity of the pending charges.

What the fuck happened in the span of twenty-four hours? The money was pouring in; the whole crew was shining and eating lovely. Shit at home with the wife wasn't perfect, but it was getting better.

Ah! man, and I got so much money and work out there in those streets, damn! I gotta stay focused. It ain't the end, of the world. I still got Prince out there to hold me down. Bad news kept pouring in.

I found out that the feds had raided my house on the Woodz and found some money, drugs, and two hammers. They also hit the stash house on the west, and struck gold, confiscating more money and drugs. When they hit the new crib, the one that I had with Sky and Skyla, they didn't find shit, because I never brought anything there.

My nerves were running wild and I was praying that they didn't know shit about Tiger, but I honestly didn't believe this case was about drugs. They're on us about all the gunplay that's been going on out here.

– County Jail –

Inside R&D, we were stripped of all our street clothing, and given tan prison garments. A nice looking sister with a fat ass and big tities started shouting out orders telling us to be quiet while she did a roll-call and told us what units we'd be going to.

Everyone except me, God, Meth and Perry were waiting to be bailed out but until then we all went to one of the holding blocks. Me, Block and God went to West-3, Meth, Cutty and Kool-Aid were taken to East-3, while Solid, Young World, and Perry went to C-3.

It was well after lockdown time, when we made it to the units, so immediately I got into my single cell, I turned in, and went right to sleep. I missed breakfast, but when the cell doors popped for recreation, I was fully awake and ready to start this thing that was called prison life. To my surprise, homies from all over Hartford came dropping off care packages.

Word had spread fast that we were in the building. Everybody was showing love, and even the opposition recognized that we were in here. Niggas we had on sight beef with just turned their cheeks and went about their business.

My nigga Shyne from the 'Ville was on my tier also. He was fighting an armed robbery case that some nigga from around his way had put on him. He said his lawyer told him to stay firm and hold tight, because the case was weak and wouldn't hold.

I quickly came to the realization that this was going to be a long, dragged out process, so I started preparing for the worst while praying for the best. My next court date wasn't for a couple of months. That gave me enough time to get my shit in order. I had to make sure I had a good lawyer, someone who would fight for me, and let me know what I am really up against.

The government was playing for keeps. The murder charges they had on me, God, and Meth were crazy, and I knew there would be other obstacles coming at us in the days to come. There was no telling what was waiting at the other end for us, but one thing was for sure –It wasn't looking too good for the home team.

I'd been in the County Jail for a few months when I peeped this fine C.O. named Ms. Jenkins, and she was watching my every move. I did some research on her and found out she'd only been working here for six months.

I knew that, given the right opportunity, I'd have her on my line in no time. With that fine ass stripper body of hers, she might be gullible enough for me to get her to smuggle some work up in here.

One afternoon during outside recreation, the majority of the inmates went out to the yard. I intentionally chose today to stay in, knowing that Ms. Jenkins was working and would be doing cell searches. Besides me, there were four other inmates who had stayed in, but they were locked in the rec room.

Ms. Jenkins was startled when she made it to my cell and found me laying on my side, across my bunk, slow-stroking my hard cock. The cheesy smile on her face told me that she was enjoying the sight.

It was a bold move I was making, but already I was dick-deep, and there wasn't any turning back. *"You coming in, or you just gonna watch?"* She came in, and I was still stroking my dick. She looked on nervously, but when I reached out to grab her hand, she moved in closer to my bunk, and grabbed hold of my hardness. She stroked me gently and said,

"Boy, you are gonna get me fired."

"Not if we get to it while we're all alone," I said.

I pulled her in for a kiss, and she kissed me back passionately. *"Hurry up and come out of that uniform."* She did as she was told. Getting behind her, I quickly inserted my dick into her cunt and rammed it until I was balls deep.

She moaned quietly as I started working back and forth, going deeper with each stroke. She was in my ear, whispering for me to go faster, and I sped up my strokes until her fat ass was smacking against my thighs.

She moaned out that she was on the verge of cumming and wanted me to cum with her. I wasn't quite ready yet, but she came hard and fast. Ms. Jenkins saw that I hadn't cum, and my rod was still rock hard. She pushed forward, causing my dick to slide out of her wet pussy.

She took me into her hands and ran her tongue up and down my cock. I let out a soft moan as she took me all the way to the hilt. She cupped my balls in her soft hands and I almost screamed out to God.

I began to move my hips to her rhythm. When my balls started to swell, she started sucking faster. The sensation was driving me crazy, up to the point when I couldn't take it anymore. My seed shot out and hit her tonsils so hard that I could hear her trying her best to swallow and not choke on my nut.

She reached out and grabbed a tissue off my desk and wiped the remaining nut from her mouth and put her clothes back on. I pulled my boxers back up and she kissed me on the lips. Ms. Jenkins thanked me and promised that she was going to make my stay in County a very enjoyable and pleasant one.

Not long after our initial sexcapade, Ms. Jenkins was wrapped around my pinky finger. She was smuggling bud, cigarettes and coke into the jail. It was funny how some good dick, a good line of talk, and a few Benjamin Franklin would completely flip a bitch.

I was a hustler by nature, so the money didn't stop just because of a federal indictment or a jail stay. The thing about prison money was, it stacked up quicker than street money.

– Work Call –

It isn't always pleasant, being locked up in prison. There was always the fact that you never knew if or when you would be a free man again. The reality of life going on and not stopping because I was now in jail stayed popping up in my head. Things in here went from zero to a hundred real quick, and this morning was a prime example of that.

"You bitch-ass nigga ...yeah, yeah ...take this, you fuckin' rat! Ya thought niggas wasn't gonna find out ya was hot!" The kid, Blaze, from Brook Street and three of his homies pushed their blades into two New Haven dudes.

Word was out that they were "hot" snitches. Things really got worse for them when one of them got some drugs on consignment and didn't pay Blaze the five-hundred-dollar tab. The dudes from New Haven were getting gutted. There was blood everywhere on the range. The walls, the floor, I mean everywhere.

The C.O. working the unit must've gone to the restroom. Once he came back and saw what was going on, he hit the code. Inmates started scattering to their cells, trying to get clear of the turmoil. Weapons were getting dumped, as evident by the sounds of toilets being flushed.

It seemed the inmates were always a step or two ahead of the officers, so by the time the block was secured; all the contraband was disposed of. There aren't any cameras in the dayroom where things popped off, so it's gonna be hard for the staff to figure out what all went down. And by looking at the work

Blaze and his crew put in, I'm sure nigga's gonna think twice about running their mouths.

Seven days later, the jail was off lockdown and everything was back to normal. I was in my cell, chilling and watching TV with a joint in my lips when I heard my name being called. I had a visit. *"Thomas! Get ready, you got a visit."*

I took a quick shower and got ready. I was thinking hard, trying to figure out who came to see me. When I got to the visiting room, I was delighted to see Queen, my mother, and Skyla. I couldn't stop smiling when I laid eyes on my two girls.

"Hey! What's up, Skyla? I miss you, princess."

"Daddy, I love and miss you too. When are you coming home?"

"Baby girl, hopefully real soon. How's things goin' at home with you and mommy? How's school?"

I had to try and change the subject and divert the conversation about her. Knowing my daughter, she will be going on and on for the rest of the visit, asking when I'm coming home. Skyla and I talked until she decided to let Queen have some phone time.

Mom Dukes asked about my case and wanted to know how I was planning to fight it. I told her that I was being forced to take the case to trial, because I was not going to cop out to a life sentence, and I definitely wasn't gonna cooperate.

The hour had come and gone and the visit was over. Just when I got up to leave the visiting room, my mother told me to sit back down, because my visit wasn't over yet. The visits were only an hour long, so I didn't know what she was thinking until Sky entered the room with the next set of visitors.

She was looking real good, wearing a yellow and white fitted Juicy Couture outfit and some all-white Air Force's on her feet. Guilt and remorse washed over me as I looked into my girl's eyes. I had violated this woman time after time, and the fact that she stayed true to me is what hurts the most. She's the mother of my child, and a good one, at that.

"Hey, Sky. How are you?"

"Hey boo. I'm good. How are you? King, I ain't gonna sit here and act like shit is good between us. It ain't and it hasn't been: I still love you, but right now I can't say that I'm gonna be here as your girl. I will not turn my back on you, and I will always be in your corner, but I need a break from us as a couple."

"Ma, I know how you're feeling right now, so whatever you choose to do, you have my blessings. Skyla is enough to get me through this."

I had to admit, this was my own doing, and I hated to see her go, but I been through more serious losses. My concentration needs to be on my case, not women. I got plenty of them. I love her and I want her to be happy; even if it ain't with me.

251

Later on, at recreation, the yard was crowded. I was on the basketball court crossing niggas over. After my visit, I desperately needed to clear my mind and forget about the fact that I was away from my family and friends.

At mail call, Ms. Jenkins was making her way from tier to tier, passing out mail. When she reached my cell door, she passed a few pieces of mail under my door along with a package that my brother Prince sent. I had to hurry up and put together a few packages for God and Meth.

We were meeting up at church at 7 p.m. Things were sweet in County. You would think we were in here doing hard time, but I was in here getting that money. After church, I rushed back to my cell to get my stinger fired up.

I fixed a Mufungo with rice, mackerel, beans, and cheese. I got a spot in line for the phone and decided to give Roxy a call. She was happy that I called. She and the kids were at home, getting ready to eat dinner. I had to admit that I really missed her. She told me she missed me too, and that she was praying for me.

I let her know I really needed all the prayers and blessings that I could get, because I had no idea how all these were going to turn out. After the call ended, I took a hot shower and got ready for bed so I could wake up in the morning and do it all over again.

Chapter Forty-One

-The Beginning of the End-

A year later, Meth, God and I were finally entering the courtroom to begin our joint trial. We were fighting counts of conspiracy to distribute crack cocaine, a murder charge pertaining to the nigga Chucky, who got merc'd, and two counts of narcotics sales to a government informant.

It was going to be an uphill battle for our lawyers, but we were ready to fight it with all that we had. The government was calling their first witness today, and that was Corry, a small-time hustler from the block. Every other one of our co-defendants copped out to count one of the indictment; with sentences ranging from 5-10 years.

Entering the courtroom flanked by federal marshals, we were all nervous and didn't really know what to expect. I could feel my heart beating extra fast as I glanced around the room to lock eyes with my family. My mother and brothers were in the front row; Shelly, Vince, and Helen were seated with them.

Roxy and Precious sat a couple of rows back. God and Meth said their hellos to everyone who was there to support them. We were all seated at the defense table, ready to fight the battle of our lives against the United States of America.

United States of America

vs.

K. Thomas, M. Wallace, G. Artist

"All rise. The Honorable Judge Andrew Fuller, presiding," announced the bailiff solemnly. Fifteen minutes later, the jurors were empanelled, and court was officially in session. *"The government calls its first witness, Corey Patterson."*

Corey walked into the courtroom, about to testify against three niggas he grew up with, niggas he'd seen better days with.

"I can't believe this bitch-ass nigga is helpin' these crackers try to send us away for the rest of our lives," I whispered to Meth.

"Mr. Patterson, can you state your full name, and where you reside, for the record," asked the Prosecutor.

"My name is Corey Patterson, and I live on Edgewood Street, on the north end of Hartford."

"Mr. Patterson, what is your occupation and what is your relationship with the Defendants?"

"Well, I don't have a real job if that's what you're asking. I sell crack cocaine on Edgewood Street. I grew up with the Defendants. We hustled on the streets together."

For the next two hours, Corey answered the Prosecutor's questions about the numerous drug transactions and shootings that took place in the 'hood. Over objections from all three lawyers, the government was able to get damaging testimony out of him. Most all of what he said were lies, but it was his story' to tell.

When it was the defense's turn, our lawyers seemed to do a good job of tearing his story apart and drilling some pretty big holes in him during cross-examination. *"You rat-ass nigga! You gonna get yours,"* Yelled several of the spectators. *"Order!"* Yelled the deep-voiced Judge, banging his gavel. *"That will not be tolerated in my courtroom!"*

Both sides finished with Corey, and the Government moved on, calling its next witness. The second witness was a complete shock to us. I never thought this nigga Chase would even show up. Word was, that he was gonna come through for us. This wasn't a good look, but shit was just gonna have to play itself out now.

My lawyer, Mr. Kubiak, said that Chase was going to testify about the robbery and about the 30G's we paid for setting up Chucky and his man. As the short, stocky man walked into the courtroom, he glanced at our table and winked at Meth.

The nigga even had the nerve to whisper, *"I got you, nigga,"* to Meth. Confused and disturbed, Meth had to be restrained from running down on Chase. Fortunately, his lawyer caught a glimpse of Meth's facial expression towards dude.

"Think twice before you make a mistake you won't be able to take back," said Meth's lawyer.

"The Government calls its second witness, Charles Reid," the Prosecutor announced. Walking towards the stand with a devilish smirk on his face, the Prosecutor introduced Charles Reid,

a.k.a., Chase. *"Mr. Reid, can you please state and spell your full name for the court?"*

"Charles Reid. C. R-E-I-D," he stated, straightening his collar.

"Mr. Reid, can you tell us why you think you are here in court today?"

"I am here to testify about three people who paid me to set someone up to be killed," Chase said.

"Okay, Mr. Reid. I want to ask you, did you indeed take payment to help set up and kill the deceased?"

"Yes, I did."

Walking closer to the jury box, the Prosecutor wound up to deliver the fatal blow: an eyewitness to the murder and an accomplice who was ready and willing to spill his guts to save his own ass, courtesy of a 5k1.1 sentence reduction, more commonly known as a "downward departure" for snitches!

"Okay, Mr. Reid, and I'm going to need you to be specific with your next answers."

"Alright," Chase replied.

"Do you see in this courtroom, the people that paid you to shoot and kill the deceased?"

A calm, arrogant witness for the Government sat up in his seat, looked into the courtroom, turned his eyes to the defense table and then spoke back to the court, *"No sir. The people that paid me ain't here right now,"* Chase said stone-faced, looking directly and intently at the Prosecutor and then the jurors.

"I don't think I heard you correctly," said a clearly perplexed Prosecutor, *"can you repeat that?"* The Prosecutor was fuming, hoping against hope, that he was mishearing what was supposed to be his star witness.

"I said, they ain't in here. I never seen them guys since that's sitting at that table before." The prosecutor exploded with rage, *"Your Honor! This witness is perjuring himself. He's recanting his previous statements and falsely testifying about not knowing the defendants."*

"No, I told you. If I see them, I'd be able to point them out. Also, when you showed me that damn photo array, I said I wasn't sure, just by looking at the pictures," Chase said defensively.

Through all of the *"oohs"* and *"ahhs"* from the spectators, the judge had to try and calm everybody down, before things got too ugly and he had to start holding people in contempt.

"Your Honor, the Government would like a twenty-minute recess," the Prosecutor pleaded. He was heated and confused. One of their best witnesses had just flipped on the stand and the very heart of their case had just stopped beating.

After the recess, shit in the courtroom was still hectic. There was a thirty-minute sidebar that went nowhere, and the Government was trying their best to figure out how to get testimony from their own witness thrown out. Through it all, it didn't seem like the Judge was trying to hear any of it.

After going back and forth on the issue for a while longer, the Judge dismissed everyone for the day and ordered both parties back in the morning to try this again. Thanks to Chase, my lawyer said there wasn't any reason to try and cross-examine him.

The way it was looking; he'd done more to help us than we could have ever anticipated. God, Meth and I said our goodbyes and I was allowed to kiss Skyla before we were shackled and hauled back off to the County.

- - -

The next day, the trial continued. Next up on the Government's list was Perry. My lawyer was extremely anxious to cross-examine him. Knowing he'd be a bit of a task, him being a rat and a liar was surely going to help us.

As usual, the courtroom was packed to capacity. The Hartford Courant was dead-smack in the middle of it all, looking for the scoop of the day. Meth, God and I were already seated at the table, dressed in various cuts of Armani. Twenty minutes later, our Attorneys came strutting into the courtroom.

Mr. Kubiac was the first one up to cross-examine Mr. Perry, and I could tell that he was in "attack mode."

"Please state your name for the record," Mr. Kubiac mocked, with the look of a lion, staring down its prey. *"Perry*

Patterson." Although Perry appeared nervous, he was still ready to help the Government bury his longtime friends. The same niggas he grew up with.

"Adversity," that's all I could think to myself. Is this really what all this shit amounted to? I found myself trying to withstand all the major blows the good niggas before me had gone through. I find myself staring into a blur as I imagined doing life, locked up in Federal prison. What was death like? Because I can't actually say which of the two I'd rather have at this point.

"Okay, now, Mr. Perry, or should I call you P? Is it correct to say that you are a known drug dealer?" Mr. Kubiac asked.

"Yes, I am," replied Perry. He said it with a confidence that'd make a motherfucker think slingin' dope was legal.

"How much drugs would you say that you've sold in your endeavors?"

"It'd be hard to put a number on it, but what I can say is that I was copping a big eight every two, three days"

"And Mr. Patterson, you testified that you would purchase these drugs from the Defendant, Mr. King Thomas?"

"Yes, I did. It wasn't just me, almost everyone from around the way copped from him," Perry said.

"Mr. Patterson, I only asked you about your dealings, not everyone else's. So, for future reference, please just answer the question I actually ask, okay?"

Mr. Kubiac was just getting started, and I could tell that Perry was already frustrated. He was twitching, as if the courtroom had him high, and he was dizzy or something.

"Now remember, Mr. Patterson, you're under oath and have sworn to tell the truth here today."

"Yes, I know."

"Do you remember testifying in front of the grand Jury to the effect that you never purchased crack cocaine from my client? And now, today, your testimony reflects and asserts that you purchased a big eight, every two or three days"

Mr. Kubiac was going in on Perry hard and exposing to the Jurors that the witness was a liar and that he couldn't be trusted. After an hour and a half, my lawyer had badgered at Perry enough, and it was now Meth's lawyer's turn. He wasted no time at all; firing off his questions at a machine gun's pace, giving Perry pure hell.

"Mr. Perry, you're a convicted felon aren't you?" Perry nodded his head shyly.

"Can you speak up and actually answer so the court can hear you?" the lawyer continued. *"Yes,"* said Perry, starting to sweat profusely. Meth's lawyer started reading over some notes and continued.

"You're in a lot of trouble, facing a life sentence." Perry fidgeted in his seat and looked at the floor.

"Mr. Patterson, are you aware that this court can charge you with perjury if you're caught lying?"

The witness nodded his head, almost choking on his own saliva when he answered, *"Yes sir."*

"Is it fair to say that you're not up to doing a life sentence in a Federal prison?"

"No," Perry replied, looking somber and wearing a silent, desperate plea on his face.

Meth's lawyer raised his voice as he asked, *"Mr. Patterson, I'm going to ask, and I want you to be careful how you respond to this, don't perjure yourself. Now, do you expect, or have you been promised anything in return for your testimony?"*

The question had the entire courtroom on the edge of its seat. Everyone could see the fear, the panic and the uncertainty in his eyes. *"The ...The prosecutor told me that if I testified against my co-defendants, he'd reduce my sentence, and I'd get to go home,"* Perry confirmed.

The crowded courtroom erupted, causing the Judge to slam his gavel again to regain order. I glanced over at the Government's table and saw the Prosecutor rub his head in frustration. He looked up at the ceiling, clearly agitated.

Meth's lawyer turned quickly to the Judge, and said, *"No further questions, your Honor."* As he strolled back to the defense table, he glanced menacingly at the Prosecutor. Understanding that our battle was still a pitched one, and knowing that the Feds played by their own set of rules, we all just stayed focused ready for our lives to be judged by twelve.

Chapter Forty-Two

A week later, after the Prosecution had put on a show with their closing arguments and our lawyers had fought to save the lives of one-time strangers. Now our lives would be connected as life and death will only come from the outcome of this high-profile case. We sat in the medals, awaiting the verdict, as the jurors deliberated.

Early Wednesday morning, I was awakened and hurried to get dressed. When I arrived downstairs, my two comrades were already waiting. The Marshals rushed us into the back of the van. After we pulled up to the Federal building, there were media vans and trucks all-over the place. Cameras were flashing as several reporters were trying to sneak questions.

I can say that for once, you could see nervousness spread across our faces. Shit, this was our lives, plus we were only human. Ten minutes later, we were seated with our lawyers. They were worn, and the depth of the trial showed on their faces. The smiles and hopeful expressions marked their real fear; that they may have failed us.

My nervous face turned into a happy, loveable one, as I looked out into the crowd, into the faces of everyone who loved me. My beautiful mother Queen, my father Nelly, my brothers, Prince, Nelly Jr., Max, Ozzy, Vince. My sister Shelly and her mom, Helen, all occupied half of the front row. Meth and God's people were mixed in amongst our loved ones.

"Daddy, daddyy! I love you," my one and only child yelled out. She sat on Sky's lap, looking just like she was cloned directly from her mother's genes. My lawyer, Mr. Kubiac, leaned over and whispered to me, *"The Jury's reached a verdict."* For the next fifteen minutes, we talked back and forth to our family members and loved ones. It was finally cut short when the Jury foreman entered the courtroom.

"Has the Jury reached a verdict?" The Judge asked.

"Yes, we have, your Honor."

Shit got serious as we looked at each other, showing strength that we would all have for life.

"Will the Defendants please stand and face the Jury?"

As I rose, I looked over to Sky and a tear almost escaped my eyes. The life I'd worked so hard to support my family was being taken away. Deep down inside, I felt a dark cloud pass over me and felt my freedom pass me by. The Jury foreman read the verdict. I blinked my eyes and my heart raced. I remembered sitting in my cell and saying that I'd rather die than spend the rest of my life in prison.

"On the first count, conspiracy to distribute crack cocaine, we find the Defendant, King Thomas, guilty."

The entire courtroom erupted in pandemonium. At that moment, I felt like I was being led to a cross, everything that was going to come after, was nails. Cries could be heard all through the courtroom. I felt no pain, no hurt; it was as if I knew all along that this would be the outcome.

The foreman cleared his throat and looked nervously around the courtroom. *"As for count two of the indictment, conspiracy to commit murder..."* This was the charge that would mean a definite life sentence in a Federal prison. *"...we find the Defendant guilty."*

Again, the room erupted, as screams and profanity and sheer hatred soared through the air. I looked over at the Prosecutor; he was salivating and giving me hard stares. I could have sworn I saw him mouth that he told me he'd get me.

With mayhem in the air, the Judge yet again pounded his gavel. Last, but not least, I was found guilty of the premeditated murder of Charles "Chucky" Reid. I was in shock and all I could do was look at my family and watch them as they wept, overcome by the verdicts.

One by one, me, then Meth, same charges, same verdicts, same outcomes. God was no different. We were all convicted on all counts. It was as if it was the day of our funerals; at least that's what it felt like. It was so hectic, that as soon as they finished God's charges, we were hauled out of there, cuffed and shackled, without even a chance to say goodbye to our loved ones.

When I got back to West-3, I was drained mentally and physically. I lied down in my single cell on top of hard steel and thought about my future. Today was a chaotic day, an eventful day.

Over and over, the Prosecutor's expression played out in my head, when Chase stated we weren't the ones who paid for the hit on Chucky. What that meant for the case was another story. The Feds played dirty, but if this was a State case, we'd be walking out the door as free men. My eyes became heavy, and I started to drift off, until I was in a deep sleep.

- - -

"King, baby! I wanna make this run to New York with you." I had a lick that was going to net me a couple hundred stacks and Roxy was demanding to take the trip with me. The lick was sweet; I had these official Queen's Bridge niggas that wanted ten bricks at twenty grand a piece.

The work was on the Grey-hound bus and on its way to the city. I rented an SUV, and me and Roxy was on I-95 heading to the big Apple to handle business, and get this money.Five hours later, and we were pulling up to Roxy's house in East Hartford.

The two suitcases we toted made it look like we were coming home from a vacation. I wheeled the suitcases into her bedroom to unload the contents. As I fumbled through the stacks of hundred dollar bills rubber-banded into Ten-G bundles, Roxy waltzed into the room wearing red thongs and some red bottom heels with no bra on.

Her breasts bounced up and down as she stepped towards the bed, hypnotizing me. Her sexy body took my mind away from the money that was scattered everywhere. Her nipples were swollen and ready to be sucked on. By this time, my cock was hard and throbbing, and ready to be released from its confinement.

As I sat on the bed, she came into my arms and kissed me. Her hands roamed my body, massaging my back and chest. She reached down and unfastened my pants as my hand found its way to her now drenched cunt. I inserted two fingers into her pussy and stroked the sensitive area of her inner core.

Roxy began to purr and had her first of many orgasms. Her pussy muscles tightened around my fingers, locking them in place. Reaching out and grabbing my cock, she guided me into her dripping wet pussy.

I started off slowly moving in and around, touching the back of her pussy until I felt what felt like walls. We were grinding into each other, melding our groins together fucking with fast, passionate movements.

Roxy mouthed that she wanted me to fuck her from the back. I rolled her lover, positioning her on all fours, and rubbed her two ass cheeks. Her heart shaped ass was slick from the love juices that dripped from her pussy, helping me ease my cock up into her.

"Oh God, King. Don't stop! You hittin' my spot." I was fucking hard and long. Roxy kept begging for more, so I gave her

just that. *"I'm cumming, King!"* My hard dick began throbbing, a sure signal that I was ready to erupt and shoot my load into her love box.

"I'm cumming, Roxy," I said out loud, but to no avail. I got no response. After a few more pumps, I felt my nut running down my own leg. *"Goddamn!"* I heard myself scream as I jumped off the bed. Looking over to my right, then over to my left, I was confused, not seeing Roxy.

I cleared my eyes for a better view, and all I saw was my 12-inch television, my locker, and other personal property that let me know I was in my cell and that I was dreaming. A fucking wet dream! *"What the hell? Please tell me that I wasn't just out there like that. This shit can't be happening!"* I whispered over and over to myself.

There's no way in hell I wasn't just 8.5 inches deep inside of Roxy's pretty, pink pussy. I even felt the crispy, hundred dollar bills sticking to my body as we were fucking. This shit is getting serious. I gotta get the hell out of here before I go crazy.

Well! A wet boxer was all I came back from that dream with. I hopped out of my bunk, located my wash towel, and some clean underclothes, laid back down, and drifted off to sleep, trying my best to chase down a dream about Highland Park.

Epilogue

King Thomas went from ballin' on the toughest basketball courts in Hartford, Connecticut to hustlin' in the grimy streets on the north end of the city. He would soon build a legacy that would be talked about in the streets for decades to come.

Standing tall by his side are his comrades, Meth and God. These three street-level hustlers were groomed and primed to become rich and famous. However, trapped in the ongoing cycle of ballin', hustlin', and the daily gunplay they had to put in, it was all that they could do to stay alive in the small, but vicious neighborhood that they came up in.

When the money really starts to pour in, the body count starts to climb at an alarming rate. That eventually causes the local authorities to call in assistance from the Federal authorities. The FBI, the DEA, and the ATF all hit the north end of Hartford and lit fire to the street's criminal activities.

In this game, many will fall; some will stand tall and, sadly, they will end up behind penitentiary walls. As the saying goes, *"Only God can judge me ... "* Soon, King, Meth and God will find out just how true that statement is. Soon, they will find out if it's God, or the Federal government who has the final say.

About the Author

King Thomas is the author of the Six Book series titled (The King of Kings). King was born in Hartford, Connecticut, but raised in Hartford and Highland Park, Michigan. He's 43 years old and the father of 2 beautiful young ladies. For the last two decades, he has been in the Fedaral Penitentiary fighting a Life sentence.

King has been through a lot in his life; in the streets and behind penitentiary walls. Through the work of fiction he's building a base with determination to give urban readers the lessons he has learned as they relate to him and so many men like himself.

CPSIA information can be obtained
at www.ICGtesting.com
Printed in the USA
LVHW080416010421
683089LV00015B/275